MOON

P9-DJA-672

FINGER LAKES

JULIE SCHWIETERT COLLAZO

DEC 2014

Contents

FINGER LAKES

This massive region, equal to New Hampshire or New Jersey in size, really seems to have it all: fascinating history, picture-perfect landscapes, farm-fresh food, and some of the country's best wines.

And that's just for starters.

According to Iroquois legend, the Finger Lakes were created when the Great Spirit reached out to bless the land, leaving imprints of his hands. Six of his fingers became the major Finger Lakes—Skaneateles, Owasco, Cayuga, Seneca, Keuka, and Canandaigua. The other four became the Little Finger Lakes—Honeoye, Canadice, Hemlock, and Conesus. He must have had an extra finger, too; that one became Otisco.

Geologists have a different creation story. They say the long, skinny parallel lakes formed from steady progressive grinding of at least two Ice Age glaciers. As the glaciers receded, lake-valleys filled with rivers that were backed by dams of glacial debris.

Depending on the weather, the water varies in hue from a deep sapphire blue to a moody gray. Along the lakes' southern edges, deep craggy gorges are sliced through the middle by silvery waterfalls. To the north are hundreds of drumlins, gentle glacier-created hills. All around lie fertile farmlands with fruit trees, buckwheat, and, especially, grapevines.

Scenic beauty is only part of the Finger Lakes story. The region's small towns abound with markers of important moments in American history. There are the homes of abolitionists Harriet Tubman and William Seward in Auburn; the National Park site

© FRANCISCO COLLAZO

HIGHLIGHTS

◖ Skaneateles Village: One of the prettiest of the Finger Lakes is anchored by this picturesque village, filled with cute shops and cafés (page 15).

◖ Women's Rights National Historical Park: The site of the first women's rights convention, organized by Elizabeth Cady Stanton and friends, met in Seneca Falls in 1848. The park has an informative visitors' center and historic sites (page 23).

◖ Wine Routes: Routes 414 and 14 are chock-a-block with wineries, with one tasting room after another tempting you inside to savor the flavor (pages 36).

◖ Watkins Glen State Park: It's hard to believe that such incredible natural beauty is so accessible to the main drag. A single turn and you're in the parking lot; two minutes later, you're at the trailhead, where you'll feel drops from the first impressive waterfall stippling your face (page 39).

◖ Mark Twain's Study: Modeled after a Mississippi steamboat pilot house, the standalone octagonal study holds the iconic writer's typewriter, hat, pipe, and other belongings (page 43).

◖ Soaring over Harris Hill: Climb into a tiny engineless glider and soar over the Seneca Lake Valley. The pilot tailors the flight to your tastes—from serene to exhilarating (page 44).

◖ Corning Museum of Glass: This remarkable collection of glass art spans over 3,000 years. Dozens of daily interactive shows and a studio where you can try your hand as a gaffer make for a fun, informative museum experience (page 46).

◖ Rockwell Museum of Western Art: This fantastic museum features an exceptional collection of painting, sculptures, photos, and multimedia work from the American West. Special children's activities make it a must-visit for families (page 47).

◖ National Museum of Play: Kids won't want to miss this sprawling children's museum, where interactive exhibits and hands-on exploration are encouraged (page 63).

◖ Boldt Castle: If you can't live in a castle that was built in tribute to you, visiting Boldt Castle—built at the bidding of George Boldt in honor of his wife—is probably the next best thing (page 79).

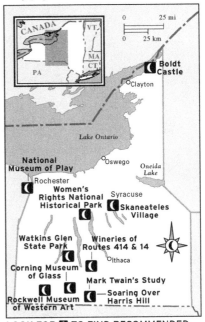

LOOK FOR ◖ TO FIND RECOMMENDED SIGHTS, ACTIVITIES, DINING, AND LODGING.

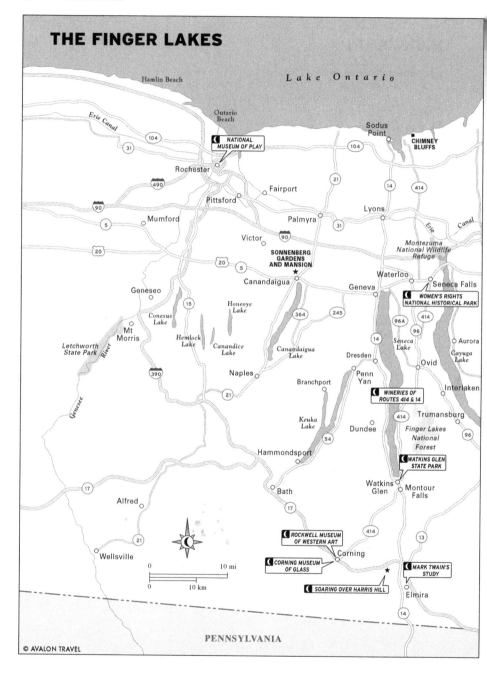

THE FINGER LAKES

Lake Ontario

Hamlin Beach

Ontario Beach

Sodus Point

■ CHIMNEY BLUFFS

Erie Canal

(NATIONAL MUSEUM OF PLAY

104

31

104

Rochester

490

21

14

414

Fairport

Pittsford

Lyons

90

Palmyra

31

Mumford

5

Victor

Erie   Canal

20

90

Montezuma National Wildlife Refuge

SONNENBERG GARDENS AND MANSION ★

Waterloo

20   5

Canandaigua

Geneva

Seneca Falls

Geneseo

(WOMEN'S RIGHTS NATIONAL HISTORICAL PARK

15

Honeoye Lake

364

245

96A   414

Conesus Lake

96

Mt Morris

Hemlock Lake

14

Seneca Lake

Aurora

Letchworth State Park

Canandice Lake

Canandaigua Lake

Dresden

Ovid

Cayuga Lake

390

Naples

Penn Yan

Interlaken

21

Branchport

(WINERIES OF ROUTES 414 & 14

414

Trumansburg

Keuka Lake

Dundee

Finger Lakes National Forest

96

54

Hammondsport

(WATKINS GLEN STATE PARK

17

Watkins Glen

Montour Falls

Alfred

Bath

17

(ROCKWELL MUSEUM OF WESTERN ART

414

13

21

Wellsville

0   10 mi

(CORNING MUSEUM OF GLASS

Corning

(MARK TWAIN'S STUDY

0   10 km

(SOARING OVER HARRIS HILL

★

Elmira

14

PENNSYLVANIA

© AVALON TRAVEL

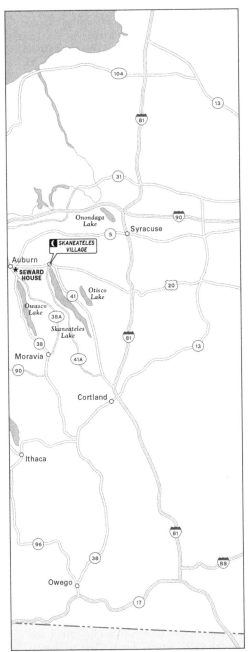

commemorating the first women's rights convention in Seneca Falls; and the Book of Mormon Historic Publication Site in tiny Palmyra, where Joseph Smith, Jr. experienced his "First Vision," leading to the establishment of the Mormon religion. The region also holds a number of interesting small cities. Syracuse was once an Erie Canal boomtown. Ithaca, home to Cornell University, is surrounded by awesome steep gorges and waterfalls.

More watery landscapes await in the Thousand Islands, an archipelago in the St. Lawrence River that separates New York and Canada. There are actually far more than 1,000—nearly 1,900 in all. Some are inhabited and can be visited, while others offer barely enough room to stand. To be counted among them, an island must be at least one square foot in size, support at least one tree, and remain above water year-round. Many scions of industry built lavish vacation homes here, including Boldt Castle, now one of the region's top tourist attractions. In the early 20th century, wealthy families from northeastern and midwestern cities would decamp to the Thousand Islands to escape the pressures of urban life and revel in the calm, unhurried pace of the islands. Despite over a century of tourism, that slower pace thankfully remains today.

PLANNING YOUR TIME

The Finger Lakes and Thousand Islands-Seaway is one of the largest regions in New York State and the distance between the two areas is considerable. Fortunately, I-90 east to I-81 north makes for a speedier connection between the Finger Lakes and the Thousand Islands-Seaway.

Given the region's size, the number of historical and natural points of interest, and the variety of wineries in the area, one could easily spend a week or two exploring the Finger Lakes and Thousand Islands. If you don't have the luxury of time, you can still experience the best of either area by training your focus on a micro-region. The Finger Lakes particularly lend themselves to settling in a single town as a home base and exploring the wineries and natural features of the lake on which that town sits.

Most travelers will probably want to start their tour in **Skaneateles,** the prettiest of the Finger Lakes, which can easily be explored in an afternoon. Just down the road is **Auburn,** home to the fascinating house-museums of abolitionists William Seward and Harriet Tubman. Beyond that is the town of **Seneca Falls,** a must stop for anyone interested in women's history.

Outdoor lovers might want to focus on the southern side of the Finger Lakes region. Here, you'll find **Ithaca,** a university town surrounded by dramatic gorges and great hiking trails; **Finger Lakes National Forest;** and, at the far western edge of the region, **Letchworth State Park,** home to the "Grand Canyon of the East." There's also the little-known Finger Lakes Trail. More than 950 miles long, it runs from the Pennsylvania-New York border in Allegany State Park to the Long Path in the Catskill Forest Preserve. Branch trails lead to Niagara Falls, the Genesee River Valley, the

Great Eastern Trail south of Corning, the central Finger Lakes, and Syracuse.

Wine lovers should focus on **Hammondsport** and **Keuka and Seneca Lakes,** which have an especially large number of vineyards, as well as lovely scenic vistas.

Culture buffs will want to spend one or two days in **Rochester,** which has an impressive children's museum and The George Eastman House, one of the finest collections of photography and film in the country. In Corning, the world-famous glass museum and Rockwell Museum of Western Art are must-sees. A visit to Corning can be paired with a stop in Watkins Glen, whose popular state park by the same name offers easy hikes with rewarding views of dramatic waterfalls and glacier-carved gorges.

The Thousand Islands are best visited in the summer months, when attractions are all open and activities are in full swing. From the Finger Lakes, you'll take I-90 east and then I-81 north to reach the region.

Syracuse

The main streets of Syracuse are oddly wide and flat, like fat rubber bands stretched out to their sides. They beg the question: who would lay out a city with so much empty space? The answer is simple. One street—Erie Boulevard—was once the Erie Canal, another, Genesee Street, was the Genesee Valley Turnpike.

Like many towns in central New York, Syracuse boomed with the opening of the Erie Canal. But long before the canal, settlers were attracted to the area for its many valuable salt springs. As early as 1797, the state took over the springs to obtain tax revenues on salt, worth so much it was referred to as "white gold."

With the opening of the Erie Canal, the salt industry developed rapidly, reaching a high point of eight million bushels a year during the Civil War. Other Syracuse industries flourished as well, including foundries and machine shops. The Irish, who had arrived to dig the

canal, remained to work the factories and were soon joined by large numbers of German immigrants. Little surprise, then, that breweries were another booming industry in Syracuse.

After the Civil War, other industries took over, among them, typewriters, ceramics, and Franklin cars, equipped with air-cooled engines. The Irish and Germans were joined by Italians, Poles, Russians, and Ukrainians.

Today, the fifth-largest city in the state (pop. 145,000) still supports a wide variety of people and industries, including National Grid, Lockheed Martin, and Syracuse University.

Orientation
The heart of Syracuse is Clinton Square, where Erie Boulevard and Genesee Street meet. The main business district lies just south of the square and is dominated by Salina and Montgomery Streets. From Clinton Square,

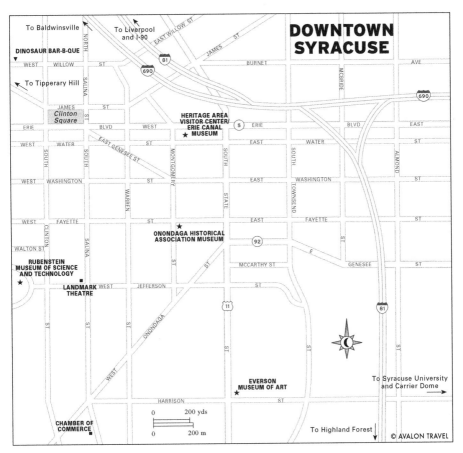

DOWNTOWN SYRACUSE

To Baldwinsville
To Liverpool and I-90
DINOSAUR BAR-B-QUE
To Tipperary Hill
Clinton Square
HERITAGE AREA VISITOR CENTER/ ERIE CANAL MUSEUM
ONONDAGA HISTORICAL ASSOCIATION MUSEUM
RUBENSTEIN MUSEUM OF SCIENCE AND TECHNOLOGY
LANDMARK THEATRE
EVERSON MUSEUM OF ART
To Syracuse University and Carrier Dome
To Highland Forest
CHAMBER OF COMMERCE
0 200 yds
0 200 m
© AVALON TRAVEL

head south on Franklin Street three blocks, and you'll find yourself in the red-brick Armory Square District, Syracuse's answer to Greenwich Village. At one end hulks the old Syracuse Armory; all around are shops, cafés, and restaurants. The district centers on the junction of Franklin and Walton Streets.

Syracuse University sits on a hill to the southeast; to the northwest is Onondaga Lake. South of the city, the sovereign 7,300-acre Onondaga Nation is home to about 750 Haudenosaunee. The Iroquois Confederacy's Grand Council of Chiefs still meets here every year, as it has for centuries.

The New York State Thruway runs east-west north of downtown. I-81 runs north-south through the center of the city. Street parking is generally available. Sights downtown are within easy walking distance of each other.

SIGHTS
Heritage Area Visitor Center and Erie Canal Museum

The long, 1850s building of the **Heritage Area Visitor Center and Erie Canal Museum** (318 Erie Blvd. E., 315/471-0593, www.erie-canalmuseum.org, Mon.-Sat. 10am-5pm, Sun. 10am-3pm, free) was once an Erie Canal weigh station for boats. Today, it's the only remaining weighlock building in the country, and it is home to a visitors center, historical exhibits, a theater where a good introductory film on the city is screened, and a 65-foot-long reconstructed canal boat. In the boat remain the original personal effects of some early passengers, including one heart-breaking letter from an Irishwoman who buried her husband at sea.

Clinton Square

Heading west two blocks from the visitors center, you'll reach **Clinton Square,** the heart of the city. The former intersection of the Erie Canal and Genesee Valley Turnpike teemed with farmers' wagons, peddlers' carts, canal boats, hawkers, musicians, and organ grinders in the old days. Today, many free outdoor events are held here.

In the mid-1800s, Clinton Square evolved from a marketplace into a financial center. Four bank buildings along Salina Street—all listed on the National Register of Historic Places— hark back to those days. Another noteworthy historic item is the four-sided, 100-foot clock tower on the 1867 Gridley Building, which was originally lit by gas jets.

At the western end of Clinton Square, near Clinton Street, stands **Jerry Rescue Monument.** The monument commemorates William "Jerry" McHenry, born into slavery in North Carolina around 1812. Jerry successfully escaped to Syracuse, where he got a job in a cooper's shop making salt barrels. He was discovered and arrested by federal marshals in 1851. A vigilante abolitionist group headed by Gerrit Smith and Dr. Samuel J. May attacked the police station and rescued Jerry, who fled to Canada a few days later. That rescue, which challenged the Fugitive Slave Act of 1850, was one of the early events precipitating the Civil War.

One block farther west on Erie Boulevard at Franklin Street is the stunning **Niagara Mohawk Power Corporation** building. Completed in 1932, the steel-and-black structure is a superb example of Art Deco architecture. The edifice is especially worth seeing at night, when it's lit by colored lights.

Rubenstein Museum of Science and Technology

The MOST, a.k.a. **Rubenstein Museum of Science and Technology** (500 S. Franklin St., 315/425-9068, www.most.org, Wed.-Sun. 10am-5pm, adults $8, seniors and children 2-11 $7), is an interactive, hands-on center that's family-friendly. Exhibit subjects include the earth, the human body, the environment, and space. Kids especially love Science Playhouse, a climbing maze, and Discovery Cave, a life-size replica of a cave, where they can learn more about cavern and fossil formation. The MOST also has a planetarium and an IMAX theater; entry to each requires a separate ticket from that presented for museum admission.

Landmark Theatre

The 2,922-seat **Landmark Theatre** (362 S. Salina St., 315/475-7980, www.landmarktheatre.org, Mon.-Fri. 10am-5pm, tours by appointment) is less than two blocks from the MOST. Designed in 1928 by Thomas Lamb, a preeminent movie-palace architect, the building's relatively sedate exterior does little to prepare you for its riotous interior—an ornate Indo-Persian fantasy rich with gold carvings. Nearly destroyed by a wrecking ball in the 1970s, the Landmark Theatre is now a beloved local institution that features traveling Broadway performances and other cultural events.

Onondaga Historical Association Museum

One of the best county museums in the state, **Onondaga Historical Association Museum** (321 Montgomery St., 315/428-1864, www.cnyhistory.org, Wed.-Fri. 10am-4pm, Sat.-Sun. 11am-4pm, free, donations welcome) covers virtually every aspect of Central New York history, from the Onondaga Nation and early African American settlers to the Erie Canal and the salt industry. Permanent exhibits include Freedom Bound: Syracuse and the Underground Railroad, Syracuse's Brewing History, and Syracuse China, which features almost 200 pieces of china made by Syracuse

China over a 130-year period. A variety of historic maps, photographs, paintings, and artifacts are also displayed.

Everson Museum of Art
Housed in a sleek, modern building designed by I. M. Pei in 1968 and widely credited for launching his career, **Everson Museum of Art** (401 Harrison St., 315/474-6064, www.everson.org, Tues.-Fri. and Sun. noon-5pm, Sat. 10am-5pm, $5 suggested donation) contains one of the world's largest collections of ceramics. The museum also displays fine collections of 19th-century American portraits, post-World War II-era photographs, and art videos from the 1960s and 1970s. Temporary exhibits often focus on contemporary American artists working in a variety of media.

Rosamond Gifford Zoo at Burnet Park
The 36-acre **Rosamond Gifford Zoo** (1 Conservation Pl., 315/435-8511, www.rosamondgiffordzoo.org, daily 10am-4:30pm, adults $8, seniors $5, students $4, children 2 and under free) on the west side of town houses about 700 animals living in recreated natural habitats, including an arctic tundra, a tropical rain forest, and an arid desert. Public overnights and meet-the-elephant opportunities are a couple of the zoo's highlights.

Tipperary Hill
West of downtown, at the juncture of West Fayette and West Genesee Streets, is the "Gateway to Tipperary Hill." Syracuse's oldest Irish neighborhood, Tipperary Hill is known for its **upside-down traffic light**, the only one in the country, at the intersection of Tompkins and Lowell Streets. When the stoplight was installed in 1925, right-side-up, members of the predominantly Irish neighborhood were irate: "British" red was placed above "Irish" green. Local boys protested by hurling stones at the light, breaking the lenses. City officials, realizing this was one battle they could never win, reversed the lenses in conciliation. Today, the green-over-red light remains and a monument to the stone throwers sits at the same intersection.

Cashel House (224 Tompkins St., 315/472-4438, www.cashelhousegifts.com), packed with goods imported from Ireland, stands in the heart of today's Tipperary Hill. Across the street, **Coleman's Authentic Irish Pub** (100 S. Lowell Ave., 315/476-1933, www.colemansirishpub.com) has been serving Irish pub grub since 1933. Look for its "leprechaun doors" as you enter and leave the restaurant.

Salt Museum
To the north, in the suburb of Liverpool, lies lozenge-shaped Onondaga Lake, whose rich salt deposits first attracted settlers to the area. The lake is currently undergoing a major clean-up to remediate pollution. To one side stands **Salt Museum** (106 Lake Dr., Liverpool, 315/453-6715, www.onondagacountyparks.com/salt-museum, early May-mid Oct. Sat.-Sun. 1pm-6pm, free), equipped with an original "boiling block." Brine was once turned into salt here through boiling and solar evaporation. Battered antique iron kettles, wooden barrels, and other equipment, along with a fascinating collection of historic photographs, are on display.

The museum and lake comprise **Onondaga Lake Park** (www.onondagacountyparks.com/onondaga-lake-park), which also offers bicycle rentals, a tram ride, a playground, and **Skä•noñh–Great Law of Peace Center** (6680 Onondaga Lake Pkwy., 315/428-1864, www.skanonhcenter.org), a second museum and heritage center on the other side of the parkway. At present, the museum itself is closed while it is repurposed from its former identity as the Ste. Marie among the Iroquois Museum. Visitors can walk the grounds during renovation, which is expected to last well into 2014.

Matilda Joslyn Gage House
History has all but forgotten Matilda Joslyn Gage, who doesn't enjoy nearly as much renown and recognition as fellow suffragettes Elizabeth Cady Stanton and Susan B. Anthony. The staff of the **Matilda Joslyn**

THE PEOPLE OF THE LONGHOUSE

When French explorers first arrived in the Finger Lakes area in the early 1600s, they found it occupied by a confederacy of five Indian nations. The French called the Indians "Iroquois"; the Indians called themselves "Haudenosaunee," or "People of the Longhouse."

The Mohawk Nation (Keepers of the Eastern Door) lived to the east of what is considered the Finger Lakes region, along Schoharie Creek and the Mohawk River Valley. The Seneca (Keepers of the Western Door) lived to the west, along the Genesee River. In the middle were the Onondaga (Keepers of the Council Fire), and it was on their territory the chiefs of the Five Nations met to establish policy and settle disputes. The two other "little brother" nations were the Cayuga, who resided between the Onondaga and the Seneca, and the Oneida, who lived between the Onondaga and the Mohawk. A sixth nation, the Tuscarora, joined the Iroquois confederacy in 1722.

During the Revolutionary War, all of the Iroquois except the Oneida sided with the British, as they had during the French and Indian War. Together with the Tories, they terrorized the pioneer villages and threatened the food supply of the Continental Army. In 1779, an angered General Washington sent Major General John Sullivan into the region, ordering him to "lay waste all the settlements around so that the country may not only be overrun but destroyed." Sullivan carried out his orders, annihilating 41 Iroquois settlements and burning many fields and orchards. By the time he was done, the Iroquois nation was in ruins. Thousands fled to Canada; others were resettled onto reservations in 1784.

Gage House (210 E. Genesee St., 315/637-9511, www.matildajoslyngage.org, hours vary seasonally), Gage's former home turned museum, is committed to doing their small part to restore Gage to history. Gage, a historian and scholar, was instrumental in drafting seminal documents of the suffrage movement; she was also an ardent abolitionist. Interestingly, she had another influence on American society as well: She was the mother-in-law of writer L. Frank Baum, famous as the author of *The Wizard of Oz*. Her life and work inspired Baum to explore the themes of courage and compassion that formed the crux of his most famous book.

At the Gage House visitors can learn a great deal about 19-century history in rooms that are devoted to the suffrage and abolition movements, as well as Iroquois influence on democracy and women's rights. There is also a room that interprets some of Baum's and Oz's history. Baum married Gage's daughter in this house and he lived here for a short time. The house is part of the National Underground Railroad Network to Freedom.

ENTERTAINMENT AND EVENTS
Performing Arts

One of the more unusual arts organizations in town is **Open Hand Theater** (518 Prospect Ave., 315/476-0466, www.openhandtheater.org), featuring giant puppets from around the world. Connected to the theater is a **Museum of International Masks and Puppets** (518 Prospect Ave., 315/476-0466, www.openhandtheater.org, by appointment), complete with hands-on activities.

Landmark Theatre (362 S. Salina St., 315/475-7980, www.landmarktheatre.org) hosts concerts, plays, dance troupes, and classic movies throughout the year.

Syracuse Stage (820 E. Genesee St., 315/443-4008, www.syracusestage.org) is the region's premier professional theater and puts on up to seven plays and musicals annually.

Red House Art Center (201 S. West St., 315/362-2785, www.theredhouse.org) is a cultural center that presents many types of work, including theater, music, and visual art, year-round.

Nightlife

The best source for what's going on where is *Syracuse New Times* (www.syracusenewtimes. com), a free alternative newsweekly published on Wednesdays, available throughout the city.

Many bars and clubs are located in the **Armory Square District** (www.armorysquare. com).

One of the liveliest music clubs in town is **Dinosaur Bar-B-Que** (246 W. Willow St., 315/476-4937, www.dinosaurbarbque.com), a friendly spot filled with dinosaurs and blues paraphernalia. Guests run the gamut from bikers to businesspeople. Live blues is performed most nights.

A good club in which to hear local bands is **Shifty's** (1401 Burnet Ave., 315/474-0048, www.shiftysbar.com), which has live music Wednesday-Sunday. On weekends, traditional Irish music can be heard at **Coleman's Authentic Irish Pub** (100 S. Lowell Ave., 315/476-1933, www.colemansirishpub.com).

Events

Syracuse Jazz Fest (www.syracusejazzfest. com) is the largest free jazz festival in the Northeast. The celebration usually runs for three days in early July, and features a wide variety of jazz events, artists, and styles. The city also hosts a smaller but growing **Blues Festival** (www.nysbluesfest.com) each summer.

One of the state's grandest parties is the **New York State Fair** (New York State Fairgrounds, 581 State Fair Blvd., Exit 7 off I-690, 315/487-7711, www.nysfair.org), featuring agricultural and livestock competitions, music and entertainment, amusement rides and games of chance, business and industrial exhibits, and talent competitions. The fair runs for 12 days, ending on Labor Day, and has attracted as many as one million visitors in past years.

SHOPPING

If there's something you forgot to pack, it would be nearly impossible not to find a replacement at **Destiny USA** (9090 Destiny USA Dr., 315/466-6000, www.destinyusa.com), a six-story shopping mall with more than 200 stores. It's the largest mall in the state and the sixth largest in the country.

SPORTS AND RECREATION

Mid-Lakes Navigation (315/685-8500, www. midlakesnav.com) offers sightseeing and dinner cruises on the Erie Canal and Skaneateles Lake. The company also offers two- and three-day cruises and has boats available for weekly rental.

Take in a Syracuse University football, basketball, or lacrosse game at the 50,000-seat **Carrier Dome** (900 Irving Ave., 315/443-4634, www.carrierdome.com).

ACCOMMODATIONS

Barrington Manor B&B (1504 James St., 315/472-7925, www.barringtonmanor.org, $99-350 d) is in a lovely residential neighborhood just east of downtown. This stately English Tudor B&B offers five attractive guest rooms filled with antiques. There's a small garden out back, and a guest kitchen is generously stocked with snacks, beer, and wine.

Comfortable **Craftsman Inn** (7300 E. Genesee St., 315/637-8000, www.craftsmaninn.com, $99-180) is in Fayetteville, 10 miles southeast of Syracuse. All 90 rooms and suites are furnished in Arts and Crafts style.

Downtown **Parkview Hotel** (713 E. Genesee St., 315/476-4212, www.theparkviewhotel. com, $129-675) is a charming boutique hotel with large, Art Deco-styled rooms. A good coffee bar, Stefon's Marketplace, also serves light meals on the first floor. The complimentary airport shuttle and free Wi-Fi add to the good value of this convenient downtown option.

Jefferson Clinton Hotel (416 S. Clinton St, 315/425-0500, www.jeffersonclintonhotel. com, $215-350), with warm, genuine service, impresses guests with little touches, from the rubber ducky atop the generous stack of bath towels to an omelet station at the complimentary breakfast buffet. Free Wii, X-Box 360, DVD and GPS rentals, Wi-Fi, and parking are added perks. What might be most winning, though, is the hotel's habit of scooting guests to their room on early arrivals whenever possible and offering free upgrades to available junior suites. The Armory Square location offers easy access to pubs, museums, and the large ice-skating pavilion during winter.

Hotel Skyler (601 S. Crouse Ave., 800/365-4663, www.hotelskyler.com, $189-399) is one of Syracuse's most interesting accommodations, built in a former temple and theater in the middle of the Syracuse University campus. The hotel's 58 rooms are decorated in a bohemian chic style, and all have free Wi-Fi. All guests enjoy complimentary access to the hotel's gym and business center, and parking is free.

Courtyard Syracuse Downtown at Armory Square (300 W. Fayette St., 315/422-4854, www.marriott.com, $199-249) opened in July 2013 in a location that is incredibly convenient to restaurants, shops, and other Syracuse attractions. The seven-story Marriott property has 96 rooms and six suites, all of which have free Wi-Fi.

FOOD

In the Armory Square District, try **Pastabilities** (311 S. Franklin St., 315/474-1153, www.pastabilities.com, Mon.-Sat. lunch and dinner, Sun. dinner, $14) for Italian fare. Also in the neighborhood, **Lemon Grass** (238 W. Jefferson St., 315/475-1111, www.lemongrasscny.com, Mon.-Sat. lunch and dinner, Sun. dinner, $20) and **Bistro Elephant Steakhouse** (238 W. Jefferson St., 315/475-1111, www.bistroelephant.com, Mon.-Sat. 5pm-close, $21) are owned by the same duo and share the same address and phone number. Lemon Grass is a Thai restaurant; Bistro Elephant is a steakhouse with some international influences.

☕ Dinosaur Bar-B-Que (246 W. Willow St., 315/476-4937, daily lunch and dinner, www.dinosaurbarbque.com, $14), known statewide for its winning sauces, is awhirl with murals of frolicking dinosaurs. Business folks on lunch breaks slip past the row of Harleys parked out front to get their 'cue on. It was ranked best BBQ in North America by *Good Morning America*. The fun, bustling hot spot serves straightforward barbecue dishes and home-style comfort foods for lunch and dinner; fried green tomatoes and pulled pork sandwiches are two favorites.

In its past life, **☕ The Mission Restaurant** (304 E. Onondaga St., 315/475-7344, www.themissionrestaurant.com, Tues.-Sun. lunch and dinner, Mon. lunch, $18) was a Methodist church, and today it still has a steeple and stained-glass windows. The church was also a stop on the Underground Railroad. Today, the repurposed building is a restaurant where Pan-American fare, with a heavy emphasis on Mexican cuisine, is served.

The Clam Bar (3914 Brewerton Rd., 315/458-1662, www.theclambarrestaurant.com, daily lunch and dinner, $18), with a deceptively 1950s kitsch, dive-ish look, complete with knotty pine walls and motorcycle parking, fronts a family-owned place touted for the best seafood in town. This claim is backed up by the crowd, which you'll want to get here early to avoid.

In Tipperary Hill, **Coleman's Authentic Irish Pub** (100 S. Lowell Ave., 315/476-1933, www.colemansirishpub.com, daily lunch and dinner, $16) is a neighborhood institution. Its menu, written in both Gaelic and English, features lots of hearty Irish fare. For Old World German food in a simple setting, try **Danzer's** (153 Ainsley Dr., 315/422-0089, $16), also a Syracuse institution, located south of downtown.

EXCURSIONS FROM SYRACUSE

Beaver Lake Nature Center

The serene, 560-acre **Beaver Lake Nature Center** (8477 East Mud Lake Rd., Baldwinsville, 315/638-2519, www.onondagacountyparks.com/beaver-lake-nature-center, daily 7:30am-dusk, $3 per car), 18 miles northwest of Syracuse, offers 9 miles of well-marked trails and boardwalks, along with a 200-acre lake that's a favorite resting spot for migrating ducks and geese. A visitors' center displays exhibits on local flora and fauna.

Highland Forest

Onondaga County's largest and oldest park is the 2,700-acre **Highland Forest** (1254 Highland Forest Rd., 315/683-5550, www.onondagacountyparks.com/highland-forest, daily dawn-dusk, $1 per person), in Fabius, about a 30-minute drive southeast of Syracuse. Spread out atop Arab Hill, the park offers great views of the surrounding countryside.

Adirondack-like in appearance, the forest is laced with four hiking trails ranging in length from less than a mile to eight miles. One-hour guided trail rides on horseback are offered May 1-October 31; hay and sleigh rides are offered on fall and winter weekends.

Green Lakes State Park

About 10 miles due east of Syracuse, 2,000-acre **Green Lakes State Park** (7900 Green Lakes Rd., Fayetteville, 315/637-6111, camping reservations 800/456-2267, www.nysparks.com/parks/172, daily dawn-dusk, $8 parking) has two aquamarine glacial lakes. Facilities include a swimming beach, hiking and biking trails, playground, campground, and 18-hole golf course. Boats can also be rented.

Camillus Erie Canal Park

Part of the much larger Erie Canalway National Heritage Corridor, **Camillus Erie Canal Park** (5750 Devoe Rd., Camillus, 315/488-3409, www.eriecanalcamillus.com) is a great place to get a sense of the significant role of the canal in the history of New York. While the **Sims Store Museum** (noon-4pm Sat. year-round, noon-4pm Wed.-Thurs. May-Oct.), modeled after an old-fashioned general store, is certainly interesting, a guided **boat tour** (1pm-5pm May-Oct.) on the canal is even more informative and engaging.

Skaneateles Lake

The farthest east of the Finger Lakes, deep blue Skaneateles is also the highest (867 feet above sea level) and most beautiful. Fifteen miles long and 1-2 miles wide, the lake is surrounded by gentle rolling hills to the south and more majestic, near-mountainous ones to the north. Iroquois for "long lake," Skaneateles is spring fed, crystal clean, and clear. In the summer, its waters are specked with sailboats; in the winter, ice fishers build igloos.

The only real village on the lake is Skaneateles. Handsome summer homes placed judicious distances apart preside elsewhere along the shoreline.

◖ SKANEATELES VILLAGE

The charming village of Skaneateles spreads out along one long main street (Route 20) at the north end of the lake. Graceful 19th-century homes, white-columned public buildings, and trim brick storefronts are everywhere and make for excellent strolling. Skaneateles has been a favorite retreat among wealthy Syracusans for generations.

The first Europeans in Skaneateles were Moravian missionaries who visited an Onondaga village here in 1750. From 1843 to 1845, the village was the short-lived site of a Utopian community that advertised in the newspapers for followers and advocated communal property, nonviolence, easy divorce, and vegetarianism. The area also served as a stopping place on the Underground Railroad, with English-born Quaker James Fuller spearheading the local abolition movement.

Clift Park, in the center of the village, is a waterfront refuge with a gazebo and wide-angled views of the lake. Docked at the end of a small pier are the two classic wooden boats of **Mid-Lakes Navigation Co.** (315/685-8500, www.midlakesnav.com, mid-May-Oct.). During warmer months, the family-owned spit-and-polish vessels offer enjoyable sightseeing, and lunch and dinner cruises. These same craft also deliver the mail on Skaneateles Lake—a 100+-year-old tradition. The knowledgeable captain offers insight into passing sights and properties, some of which her family settled generations before.

The Creamery

To learn about the lake's history, step into **The Creamery** (28 Hannum St., 315/685-1360, www.skaneateleshistoricalsociety.org, Nov.-Apr. Fri. 1pm-4pm, May-Oct. Fri.-Sat. 1pm-4pm, donations welcome), a small, local museum housed in the former Skaneateles Creamery building. From 1899 to 1949, area farmers brought their milk here to be turned into buttermilk, cream, and butter. Displays include scale models of the boats that once sailed the lake, exhibits on dairy farming, and information about the teasel, a thistle-like plant once used in woolen mills to raise a cloth's nap. For 120 years, Skaneateles was the teasel-growing capital of the United States. The Creamery is run by the **Skaneateles Historical Society** (28 Hannum St., 315/685-1360, www.skaneateleshistoricalsociety.org), which also offers walking tours of the village.

New Hope Mills

For spectacular views of the lake, drive down either Route 41 to the east or Route 41A to the west. Route 41A veers away from the shoreline at the southern end and leads to **New Hope Mills** (181 York St., Auburn, 315/252-2676, www.newhopemills.com, Mon.-Fri. 8am-4pm, Sat. 10am-2pm), an 1823 flour mill that is currently being converted into a museum. Unbleached flours and grains are for sale in the mill's store, and coffee and baked goods are served in the café.

Events

Weekly **sailboat races** (2745 East Lake Rd., www.skansailclub.com, June-Aug. Wed. 5:30pm, Sat.-Sun. 2pm) take place throughout the summer, while free **band concerts** (W. Genesee St., across from the Sherwood Inn, www.skaneateles.com, July Fri. 7:30pm, Aug. Fri. 7pm) are held on Friday evenings in Clift Park. **Polo games** are played on Sunday afternoons in July and August at **Skaneateles Polo**

Club (783 Andrews Rd., 315/685-8545). Since 1980, the **Skaneateles Festival** (www.skanfest.org) has been bringing top chamber-music artists to town in August. The town's largest event is the **antique and classic boat show** (north end of Lake Skaneateles, 315/685-0552, www.skaneateles.com) in early July.

But not all of the fun happens in the summer. The cold weather brings what Skaneateles calls "the world's smallest Christmas parade": Scrooge, Bob Cratchit, Tiny Tim, and a handful of other characters from Charles Dickens' *A Christmas Carol* kick off holiday festivities with a march around town. **Dickens Christmas** (www.skaneateles.com) celebrated its 20th anniversary in 2013. Beloved by locals and visitors alike, the festival features free horse and carriage rides, free roasted chestnuts, and free hot cider and donuts (or hot chocolate served by village Girl Scouts). There's also caroling on most every street corner, a sing-along in the village gazebo, Mother Goose story-time, and Father Christmas giving out free treats for the best little visitors. Live Dickens characters interact with townsfolk and visitors in the shops and along the streets and perform scenes from the Dickens classic. It's enough to warm the cockles of the Scrooge-iest visitor's heart.

Accommodations

Across from the park is the hospitable **C Sherwood Inn** (26 W. Genesee St., 315/685-3405, www.thesherwoodinn.com, $185-295), a rambling, colonial blue building that was once a stagecoach stop. The inn was established in 1807 by Isaac Sherwood, a man who began his career by delivering the mail on foot between Utica and Canandaigua and ended it as the "stagecoach king." Upscale yet casual, the inn includes a very popular restaurant, a tavern with frequent live entertainment, and 25 attractive guest rooms, all decorated with antiques. Contributing to the inn's relaxed atmosphere are a big screened-in porch with wonderful views of the lake, an outdoor patio for summer dining, lots of fresh flowers, and a snug lounge.

The Gray House (47 Jordan St., 315/685-0131, www.gray-house.com, $99-185), near the heart of downtown, is a welcoming B&B housed in a spacious Victorian home. It has five guest rooms, a large parlor, two breezy porches, and gardens.

Hobbit Hollow Farm (3061 West Lake Rd., 315/685-2791, www.hobbithollow.com, $100-170), a century-old colonial Revival farmhouse, overlooks Skaneateles Lake from its picturesque 400-acre perch. This four-season property offers a full country breakfast, afternoon wine and cheese tasting, Wi-Fi, spa robes, snowshoes, and private baths.

Ultra-luxurious **Mirbeau Inn and Spa** (851 W. Genesee St., 315/685-5006 or 877/647-2328, www.mirbeau.com, $185-385) is on the outskirts of Skaneateles. The elegant, European-style inn, complete with wall frescoes, waterfalls, soft lighting, and 18 spacious guest rooms, also has an on-site spa. The inn is also known for its serene restaurant.

Food

The laid-back ⟨ **Doug's Fish Fry** (8 Jordan St., 315/685-3288, www.dougsfishfry.com, daily lunch and dinner, $12) is a local favorite, renowned for its chowder, fried scallops, gumbo, and fish sandwiches.

Rosalie's Cucina (841 W. Genesee St., 315/685-2200, www.rosaliescucina.com, $27) offers first-rate Italian fare, ranging from pizza and pasta to grilled lobster tails, in an adobe tavern.

In addition to great accommodations, Sherwood Inn and Mirbeau Inn both have excellent restaurants. The restaurant at **Mirbeau** (851 W. Genesee St., 315/685-5006 or 877/647-2328, www.mirbeau.com, daily breakfast, lunch, and dinner, $32) serves creative American cuisine made with fresh local ingredients. Mirbeau also hosts special dinners with visiting chefs and special guests as well as cooking classes. The restaurant at **Sherwood Inn** (26 W. Genesee St., 315/685-3405, www.thesherwoodinn.com, $26) features traditional American fare. Check out **Patisserie** (4 Hannum St., 315/685-2433), which provides all the breads for the Sherwood Inn, a perfect stop for a great morning coffee and pastry.

Independent bookshop and café **Creekside Books and Coffee** (35 Fennell St., 315/685-0379, www.creeksidecoffeehouse.com) is a great place to stop for an espresso or glass of wine while leisurely browsing books. The café hosts wine tastings, author readings, cooking demos, and live music in a cozy, bookish atmosphere.

CORTLAND

About 12 miles from the southern tip of Skaneateles Lake sprawls the city of Cortland (pop. 19,292). Set in the midst of fertile farm country, Cortland was once a small industrial center, best known for its wire cloth, lingerie, and corset factories. A **National Historic District** of handsome homes and commercial buildings is found on Main Street between Tompkins Street and Clinton Avenue.

Cortland also has a claim to literary fame. It was here that Chester Gillette, the real-life counterpart to the character Clyde Griffiths in Theodore Dreiser's *An American Tragedy*, met Grace Brown. Writes Dreiser of Griffiths's arrival in his new hometown: "He found himself ambling on and on until suddenly he was...in touch with a wide and tree-shaded thoroughfare of residences, the houses of which, each and every one, appeared to possess more room space, lawn space, general ease and repose and dignity even than any with which he had ever been in contact...." Gillette once worked in his uncle's Gillette Skirt Factory on the north side of town, and lived in the double house at No. 17 East Main Street, which stands today.

1890 House Museum

Perhaps one of the houses spotted by Gillette/Griffiths in his ramble was the castle-like **1890 House Museum** (37 Tompkins St., 607/756-7551, www.the1890house.org, year-round Thurs.-Sat. noon-4pm, adults $8, seniors and students $5, children under 10 free), built by wire manufacturer Chester F. Wickwire. Now an informal museum, the house holds 30 rooms notable for their parquet floors, stained-glass windows, ornate stenciling, and hand-carved woodwork. A tower provides excellent views of the town. Walking-tour maps of Cortland's Historic District can be picked up here.

Cortland Country Music Park

Part RV camp, part country-music mecca, the 18-acre **Cortland Country Music Park** (1824 Rte. 13, 607/753-0377, www.cortlandmusicpark.com) bills itself as the "great Nashville of the Northeast." During summer, four or five concerts by top performers are staged, along with two-steppin' dance classes, square dances, and jamborees. The park offers live music by regional bands on weekends year-round and special events including horseshoe tournaments, the Old Timers Show, and the Festival of Bands.

The music park, which was built by volunteer country music fans, started in 1975. Centered around an Opry barn, it is equipped with one of the largest dance floors in the Northeast, an outdoor stage, and a Hall of Fame Museum (open only during events). In the museum, you'll find everything from a black-sequined dress formerly owned by Tammy Wynette to white boots once worn by Roy Acuff.

Shopping

It's worth traveling about eight miles south of Cortland to visit the **Book Barn of the Finger Lakes** (198 North Rd., Dryden, 607/844-9365, Mon.-Sat. 10am-5:30 pm, Sun. noon-5pm). The complex, which actually consists of three barns, houses 2.5 miles of shelves laden with nearly 100,000 books in 254 categories. It is run by Vladimer Dragan, who buys and sells all his books in person, even making house calls to estates and libraries.

Accommodations

Greek Peak Mountain Resort and Hope Lake Lodge and Indoor Waterpark (2000 Rte. 392, 800/955-2754, www.greekpeak.net, $340 fireplace suite for 2-4 people) is a four-season resort catering to skiers, families, and spa lovers. There are waterpark-inclusive packages and accommodations tailored to guests' individual interests. The resort offers several cafés and restaurants, 32 ski trails, a tubing center, and Nordic skiing and snowshoeing. Full service Waterfalls Spa gives non-snowbunnies plenty of treatments to enjoy.

Owasco Lake

The smallest of the major Finger Lakes, Owasco is 12 miles long and 1.5 miles wide at its widest point. Iroquois for "the crossing," Owasco lies 720 feet above sea level. For great views of the lake, take Route 38 south, hugging the western shore, or Route 38A south, which travels high above the lake to the east. A few miles down, Route 38A bumps into Rockefeller Road, a shoreline route lined with 150-year-old camps and houses.

The city of Auburn, population 27,365, sits at the northern end of Owasco. At the southern end are the village of Moravia, birthplace of President Millard Fillmore, the Fillmore Glen State Park, and miles of farm country.

AUBURN

For a small city, Auburn has been home to an unusually high number of remarkable men

and women: Logan, or Tahgahjute, Iroquois orator; Harriet Tubman, African American leader; William H. Seward, visionary statesman; Thomas Mott Osborne, pioneer of prison reform; and Theodore W. Case, the inventor of sound film. Tributes to all can be found in the city.

Auburn was originally a Cayuga Indian village established at the junction of two trails. Revolutionary War veteran Colonel John Hardenbergh arrived in 1793 and built the area's first gristmill. By 1810, the village boasted 90 dwellings, 17 mills, and an incorporated library containing 200 books.

The opening of the Auburn State Prison in 1817 and the Auburn Theological Seminary in 1821 greatly stimulated growth. By the mid-1800s, Auburn was thriving. It even

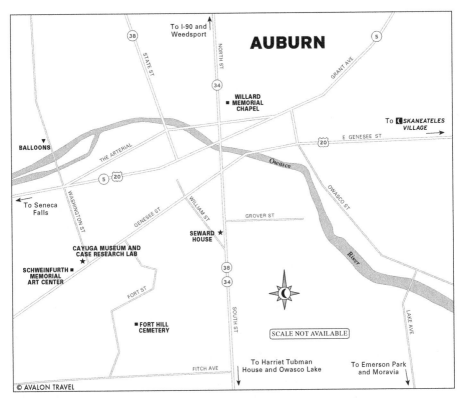

entertained hopes of becoming the state capital. The impressive public buildings on Genesee Street and lavish private homes on South Street date back to those heady days.

Seward House

One of the most interesting house museums in New York is **Seward House** (33 South St., 315/252-1283, www.sewardhouse.org, June-Labor Day Tues.-Sat. 10am-5pm and Sun. 1pm-5pm, hours vary off-season, closed Jan.-Feb., adults $8, seniors $7, students $5, children under 6 free), a stately 1816 Federal-style home shaded by leafy trees. The house belonged to William H. Seward, ardent abolitionist, New York governor, and U.S. senator, best remembered for purchasing Alaska from the Russians in 1857. Seward also served as Lincoln's secretary of state and was almost assassinated by a co-conspirator of John Wilkes Booth at the same time as the president.

Amazingly, almost everything in the Seward house is original. Inside, you'll find not only Seward's furniture, but his grocery bills, top hats, pipe collection, snuff-box collection, 10,000 books, political campaign buttons, tea from the Boston Tea Party, personal letters from Abraham Lincoln, and calling cards of former visitors Horace Greeley, Frederick Douglass, Millard Fillmore, and Daniel Webster.

Seward first moved to Auburn for the love of Miss Frances Miller, whose father, Judge Elijah Miller, built the house. As a newly minted lawyer, Seward got a job in the judge's law firm and proposed to his daughter. The ornery judge allowed the liaison on one condition: Seward could never take his daughter away from him.

Seward agreed and, despite his enormous worldly success, lived under his father-in-law's thumb for the next 27 years.

Excellent guides bring the past alive and a fascinating collection of visiting leaders makes for a fun "Guess Who" game. Perhaps the most interesting aspect of the museum is the revelation and proof, in the form of photographs, news clippings, an eyewitness account, and a bloodied, rent garment, that Lincoln was not a solo target that fateful night in the theater.

Harriet Tubman Home

On the outskirts of Auburn, next door to the AME Zion Church, stands the **Harriet Tubman Home** (180 South St., 315/252-2081, www.harriethouse.org, Tues.-Fri. 10am-4pm, Sat. 10am-3pm, adults $4.50, seniors $3, children $1.50), comprised of a brick house and adjacent white clapboard house wrapped with a long front porch. Known as the "Moses of her people," Harriet Tubman settled here after the Civil War, largely because her close friend and fellow abolitionist William Seward lived nearby.

Born a slave in Maryland in 1820 or 1821, Tubman escaped in 1849, fleeing first to Philadelphia and then to Canada. Yet as long as others remained in captivity, her freedom meant little to her. During the next dozen years, she risked 19 trips south, rescuing more than 300 slaves. She mostly traveled alone and at night. Her motto was "Keep going; children, if you are tired, keep going; if you are scared, keep going; if you are hungry, keep going; if you want to taste freedom, keep going."

A visit to the Tubman property begins in the Visitor Center with interpretive panels that follow the timeline of Tubman's life and pertinent events. Afterward, a member of the AME Zion Church takes visitors on a tour of the clapboard house where Tubman tended to the elderly and where a few of her belongings, including her bed and Bible, are on display. Tubman herself lived in the brick house. Though not open at present, there are future plans to make the house accessible to the public.

Fort Hill Cemetery

Harriet Tubman, William Seward, and numerous other Auburn notables are buried in **Fort Hill Cemetery** (19 Fort St., 315/253-8132, www.cayuganet.org/forthill, Mon.-Fri. 9am-4pm), on a hill to the west side of South Street. Native Americans used the site as burial grounds as early as AD 1100.

A large stone fortress-gate marks the cemetery entrance; inside towers the 56-foot-high **Logan Monument.** Erected upon a mound believed to be an ancient Native American altar, the monument pays homage to Logan, or Tahgahjute, the famed Cayuga orator born near Auburn in 1727. Logan befriended European settlers until 1774, when a group of marauding Englishmen massacred his entire family in the Ohio Valley. In retaliation, he scalped more than 30 white men. Later that same year in Virginia, at a conference with the British, he gave one of the most moving speeches in early American history. "Logan never felt fear," he said. "He will not turn his heel to save his life. Who is there to mourn for Logan? Not one."

Cayuga Museum and Case Research Lab

Housed in a Greek Revival mansion, **Cayuga Museum** (203 Genesee St., 315/253-8051, www.cayugamuseum.org, Feb.-Dec. Tues.-Sun. noon-5pm, suggested donation $3) is devoted to local history. Exhibits cover early Native American culture, the Civil War, the Auburn Correctional Facility, Millard Fillmore, and women's rights.

Behind the museum mansion stands a simple, low-slung building known as the **Case Research Lab** (203 Genesee St., 315/253-8051, www.cayugamuseum.org, Feb.-Dec. Tues.-Sun. noon-5pm, suggested donation $3). Here, in 1923, Theodore W. Case and E. I. Sponable invented the first commercially successful sound film, ushering in the talking movie era. Displays include the first sound camera and projector, original lab equipment, and Case's correspondence with Thomas Edison and Lee De Forest, a self-promoter who claimed *he* was the inventor of sound film.

Schweinfurth Memorial Art Center

Next to the Cayuga Museum, **Schweinfurth Memorial Art Center** (205 Genesee St., 315/255-1553, www.schweinfurthartcenter.org, Tues.-Sat. 10am-5pm, Sun. 1pm-5pm, closed between exhibits, adults $6, children 12 and under free) features temporary exhibits by contemporary and classic artists. Shows feature everything from fine art and photography to folk art and architecture. Each winter the museum hosts a popular juried quilt show.

Willard Memorial Chapel

The only complete and unaltered Tiffany chapel known to exist, **Willard Memorial Chapel** (17 Nelson St., 315/252-0339, www.willard-chapel.org, Feb.-Dec. Tues.-Fri. 10am-4pm, Jan. Thurs.-Fri. 10am-4pm, $5) glows with the muted, bejeweled light of 15 windows handcrafted by Tiffany Glass and Decorating Company. Louis C. Tiffany also designed the chapel's handsome oak furniture, inlaid with mosaics, leaded-glass chandeliers, and gold-stenciled pulpit.

A visit to the chapel begins with a video on the chapel's history and the now-defunct Auburn Theological Seminary of which it was once a part. In July and August, free organ recitals and concerts are played in the chapel.

Accommodations and Food

One mile south of Auburn you'll find **Springside Inn** (6141 W. Lake Rd., 315/252-7247, www.springsideinn.com, $100-250, with continental breakfast), a striking red Victorian with big white porches. Upstairs are seven guest rooms furnished with antiques and nice touches like canopy beds and claw-foot or whirlpool tubs.

The Springside Inn is well known for its modern gastropub, **Oak & Vine** (6141 W. Lake Rd., 315/252-7247, www.oakandvine.com, Mon.-Sat. dinner, Sun. brunch, $22), a local favorite for special occasions. The menu features American cuisine, including organic pasta and locally sourced organic produce.

Balloons (67 Washington St., across from the state prison, 315/252-9761, www.balloonsrestaurant.net, Tues.-Sat. dinner, $14) is a friendly spot with Art Deco decor, serving heaping platters of Italian-American food since 1934.

The Restaurant at Elderberry Pond (3712 Center Street Rd., 315/252-6025, www.elderberrypond.com, mid-Mar.-Dec. Wed.-Sun. lunch and dinner, $30) is surrounded by 100 acres of organic ingredients, from herbs to free range meats, grown right on Elderberry Pond Farm. The menu changes daily; a sampling includes items like organic whole wheat pasta served with an assortment of daily garden pickings. The adjacent farm store, located in an 1800s smokehouse, is a good spot to pick up some favorites for the road.

MORAVIA

At the southern end of Owasco Lake is Moravia, birthplace of President Millard Fillmore. Well off the beaten track, this small village boasts a number of handsome 19th-century buildings and the 1820s **St. Matthew's Episcopal Church** (14 Church St., 315/497-1171, Mon.-Fri. 8am-5pm, tours by appointment). The sanctuary's interior is covered with elaborate oak carvings designed and executed in Oberammergau, Germany.

FILLMORE GLEN STATE PARK

Just south of Moravia lies the 857-acre **Fillmore Glen State Park** (1686 Rte. 38, 315/497-0130, camping reservations 800/456-2267, www.nysparks.com/parks/157, daily dawn-dusk, $7 parking), centered on a deep, rugged ravine with five spectacular waterfalls. At the foot of the main falls is a geometric rock formation known as the Cowpens, and a popular swimming hole. Nearby are hiking trails, a campground, and a playground.

The park also contains a replica of the tiny log cabin in which President Millard Fillmore was born. His actual birthplace lies about five miles east of the park. Fillmore grew up dirt poor and went to work at an early age; he later described his upbringing as "completely shut out from the enterprises of civilization and advancement."

Cayuga Lake

The longest of the Finger Lakes, Cayuga stretches out for just under 40 moody miles, 382 feet above sea level. It varies in depth from a few feet to 435 feet, and supports a wide variety of marine life, with carp and large-mouth bass swimming in shallow waters and northern pike and lake trout inhabiting deeper ones.

Cayuga was named after the Iroquois nation that originally lived along its shores (the literal translation of Cayuga is "boat landing"). The Cayugas were called Gue-u-gweh-o-no, or people of the muckland, exemplified by the once-enormous Montezuma Marsh at the northern end of the lake.

Seneca Falls, the small industrial town where the first Women's Rights Convention met in 1848, sits just south of the marsh. Anchoring the southern end of the lake is Ithaca, a friendly cultural center that's home to Cornell University, Ithaca College, and craggy gorges with waterfalls higher than Niagara. Along the lake's eastern and western shores are approximately 20 wineries; on the eastern shore is the historic village of Aurora.

SENECA FALLS

Seneca Falls owes its early development to a series of waterfalls dropping over 50 feet. The first gristmill was built here in 1795, and by the 1840s, the town supported dozens of water-powered factories. Many employed women worked 14-hour days for wages they had to turn over to their husbands. In 19th-century America, women were not allowed to own money or property or to even serve as legal guardians of their own children. This was the environment in which Elizabeth Cady Stanton gathered the historic 1848 convention that issued a Declaration of Sentiments calling for greater rights for women.

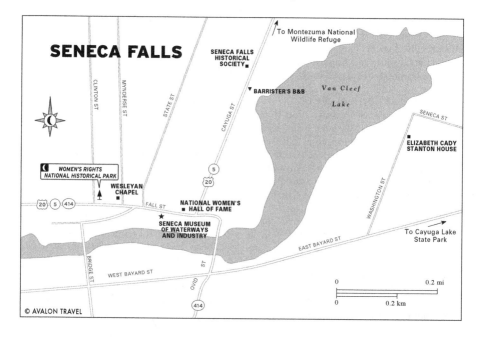

Today, Seneca Falls centers around Fall Street (Rtes. 5 and 20). Running parallel to Fall Street is the Seneca River and the Cayuga-Seneca Canal, which links Cayuga and Seneca Lakes. At the eastern end of town is the artificially constructed Van Cleef Lake.

Heritage Area Visitors Center

For a good general introduction to Seneca Falls, stop into the **Heritage Area Visitors Center** (115 Fall St., 315/568-1510, Mon.-Sat. 10am-4pm, Sun. noon-4pm, free). The exhibits cover virtually every aspect of the town's history, from its Iroquois beginnings and early factory days to its women's history and ethnic heritage, as well as the area's industrial past. Seneca Falls once held world fame for its knitting mills and pump factories.

Don't leave the center without learning about the destruction of the city's once invaluable waterfalls. The falls were eliminated in 1915 to create the Cayuga-Seneca Canal and, by extension, Van Cleef Lake. The flooding destroyed more than 150 buildings; today, many foundations are still visible beneath the lake's clear waters.

◖ Women's Rights National Historical Park

Elizabeth Cady Stanton and her abolitionist husband Henry Stanton moved to Seneca Falls from Boston in 1847, a time when the town was both a major transportation hub and a center for the abolitionist movement. Often home alone, caring for her children, Stanton felt isolated and overwhelmed by housework. She also noticed the plight of her poorer neighbors: "Alas! alas!," she wrote in her autobiography *Eighty Years and More,* "Who can measure the mountains of sorrow and suffering endured in unwelcome motherhood in the abodes of ignorance, poverty, and vice...."

On July 13, 1848, Stanton shared her discontent with four friends. Then and there, the group decided to convene a discussion on the status of women. They set a date for six days thence and published announcements in the local papers. About 300 people—men

and women—showed up. During the meeting, the group's Declaration of Sentiments was issued, calling for greater rights for women. Stanton and her friends deemed the convention a success. They were little prepared for the nationwide storm of outrage and ridicule that followed. Their lives, the town of Seneca Falls, and the nation would never be the same.

Wesleyan Chapel (126 Fall St.), where the historic 1848 convention took place, still stands. However, the structure is not entirely original. After suffering decades of weathering and vandalism, most of the chapel was in ruins. A restoration project improved the exterior, providing protection for some of the original elements of the architecture; National Park Service rangers now lead guests on tours of the chapel.

Nearby is a 140-foot-long wall and fountain inscribed with the Declaration of Sentiments: "We hold these truths to be self-evident; that all men and women are created equal...."

Next to the wall is the spacious, two-story **Visitor Center** (136 Fall St., 315/568-2991, www.nps.gov/wori, daily 9am-5pm, free), managed by the National Park Service. Here, you'll find exhibits on the convention, its leaders, and the times in which they lived. Other sections focus on employment, marriage, fashion, and sports. There's a lot of interesting information, along with free handouts and a good bookstore.

Elizabeth Cady Stanton House

Elizabeth Cady Stanton House (32 Washington St., tours June-Sept. daily, $1 pp) is about a mile from the visitors center on the other side of Van Cleef Lake. Stanton lived here with her husband and seven children from 1846 to 1862. During much of that time, she wrote extensively about women's rights.

Among the many reformers who frequented the Stanton home was Amelia Bloomer, the woman who popularized the clothing that bears her name. Though a resident of Seneca Falls, Bloomer did not sign the Declaration of Sentiments, believing it to be too radical.

The meticulously restored Stanton House is full of authentic, original ephemera from

Stanton's life and era, including the bronze cast of Stanton's hand clasping that of Susan B. Anthony. Stanton met Anthony soon after the 1848 convention, and the women worked closely together throughout their lives.

In summer months, **house tours** are offered daily; visitors must sign up for the tours at the Women's Rights Visitor Center (136 Fall St., 315/568-2991).

Seneca Museum of Waterways and Industry

Housed in a historic building, the **Seneca Museum of Waterways and Industry** (89 Fall St., 315/568-1510, www.senecamuseum.com, Sept.-mid-June Tues.-Sat. 10am-4pm, mid-June-Aug. Tues.-Sat. 10am-4pm and Sun. noon-4pm, adults $2, families $5) is filled with exhibits on the history of the village and its surrounding waterways. A colorful 35-foot mural lines one wall. The museum has antique fire engines, pumps, looms, and printing presses. One exhibit shows how the Erie Canal was built, another is a working lock model.

National Women's Hall of Fame

The **National Women's Hall of Fame** (76 Fall St., 315/568-8060, www.greatwomen.org, Sept.-May Wed.-Sat. 10am-4pm, June-Aug. Wed.-Sat. 10am-4pm and Sun. noon-4pm, adults $3, seniors and students $1.50, children under 5 free) bills itself as "the only national membership organization devoted exclusively to the accomplishments of American women." Enlarged photos and plaques pay homage to everyone from painter Mary Cassatt to anthropologist Margaret Mead.

Seneca Falls Historical Society

Seneca Falls Historical Society (55 Cayuga St., 315/568-8412, www.sfhistoricalsociety. org, Mon.-Fri. 9am-4pm, adults $7, students $5, families $20) is housed in a notable Queen Anne home, set back from the street behind an iron fence. Inside, 23 elegant rooms feature period furnishings, elaborate woodwork, and an extensive costume collection. A rare collection of 19th-century circus toys is strewn through the children's playroom.

Montezuma Audubon Center

Five miles east of Seneca Falls is the **Montezuma Audubon Center** (2295 Rte. 89, Savannah, 315/365-3580, www.ny.audubon. org/montezuma, Apr.-Nov. daily dawn-dusk, free), a haven for migrating and nesting birds. Spread out over 6,300 acres of swamplands, marshlands, and fields, the refuge includes a visitors' center, nature trail, driving trail, and two observation towers. Nearly 315 species of birds have been spotted in the refuge since it was established in 1937. Migrating waterfowl arrive by the tens of thousands in mid-April and early October. Late May to early June is a good time to spot warblers; in mid-September, the refuge fills with shorebirds and wading birds.

Before the turn of the century, Montezuma Marsh was many times its current size, stretching about 12 miles long and up to 8 miles wide. The Erie Canal and Cayuga Lake dam projects greatly reduced its size.

Cayuga Lake State Park

Three miles east of Seneca Falls lies the 190-acre **Cayuga Lake State Park** (2678 Lower Lake Rd., 315/568-5163, camping reservations 800/456-2267, www.nysparks.com/parks/123, daily dawn-dusk, parking $6-8), offering a swimming beach, a bathhouse, hiking trails, a playground, and a 287-site campground. In the late 1700s, the park was part of a Cayuga Indian reservation, and in the late 1800s it was a resort area serviced by a train from Seneca Falls. The state park was established here in 1928.

Finger Lakes National Forest

The 16,212-acre **Finger Lakes National Forest** (National Forest Headquarters, 5218 Rte. 414 Hector, 607/546-4470, www.fs.usda.gov/fingerlakes) lies between Seneca and Cayuga Lakes and is the state's sole National Forest. Gorges, woods, pastures, shrub lands, and many wildlife ponds are intermingled to provide excellent opportunities for wildlife viewing and fishing. Over 30 miles of trails, including the 12-mile Interloken Trail, part of the **Finger Lakes Trail,** allow for hiking and horseback riding in the warm months and snowmobiling and skiing in the winter. Apples, raspberries, and other fruits are abundant throughout the forest, with five acres managed specifically for blueberry bushes. Free camping is available on three developed campgrounds on a first-come, first-served basis.

Events

Convention Days Celebration (315/568-8060, www.conventiondays.com), commemorating the first Women's Rights Convention, takes place each year on the weekend closest to July 19-20. Concerts, dances, speeches, historical tours, food, kids' events, and a reenactment of the signing of the Declaration of Sentiments form the schedule of activities.

Accommodations and Food

Several lovely B&Bs are in the heart of Seneca Falls. The 1855 **Hubbell House** (42 Cayuga St., 315/568-9690, www.hubbellhousebb. com, $155-300), built in Gothic cottage style, overlooks Van Cleef Lake. Downstairs are a large double parlor, library, and dining room; upstairs are four guest rooms furnished with antiques.

The large, historic (**Barristers Bed and Breakfast** (56 Cayuga St., 800/914-0145, www.sleepbarristers.com, $159-179), built by master craftsmen in the 1800s, features five spacious guest rooms furnished with antiques, a large front porch, cozy common room, and stone patio with a fire pit, perfect for sitting around on cool evenings. Guest amenities include a refreshment center.

The fresh, modern **Gould Hotel** (108 Fall St., 315/712-4000, www.thegouldhotel.com, $99-189) offers 48 rooms and suites with clean contemporary lines and extensive amenities (robes, Keurig coffee machines, iPod docking stations). The excellent **Restaurant at the Gould Hotel** (average entrée $22) and a hipster-ish bar experience await downstairs.

Don't call it "just" a grocery store: **Wegmans** (1 Loop Rd., Auburn, 315/255-2231, www.wegmans.com, open 24 hours daily) is a local institution. Visitors come to love it too because of sprawling hot and cold buffet bars, with a wide array of options for a quick, delicious, and healthy lunch.

WATERLOO

A few miles west of Seneca Falls on Routes 5 and 20 is Waterloo, a surprisingly busy village filled with aging red-brick buildings and shady trees. As a plaque along Main Street attests, Waterloo claims to be the birthplace of Memorial Day. Originally known as Declaration Day, the event apparently first took place here on May 5, 1866, in honor of the Civil War dead. Flags flew at half-mast, businesses closed, and a solemn parade marched down Main Street. In 1966, Congress and President Johnson officially recognized Waterloo as the birthplace of Memorial Day.

In the middle of town you'll find **Terwilliger Museum** (31 E. Williams St., 315/539-0533, Tues.-Fri. 1pm-4pm), which has a reconstructed Native American longhouse and village store, along with antique pianos, carriages, fire equipment, and a 1914 Waterloo mural.

You can also rent kayaks, canoes, and campsites from **Canal Side Experiences** (706 Waterloo-Geneva Rd., 315/651-4443, www.canalside.net). If you prefer that someone else take the helm, you can hire them to take you on a canal excursion on one of their pontoon boats. The quirky one-stop-shop also offers shopping, snacks, and entertainment. The owners operate a paint-your-own-pottery studio and rent time on their radio-controlled "theme park" with cars, trucks, and tanks you can drive around a homemade obstacle course.

Also on the canal, **Fuzzy Guppies** (1278 Waterloo-Geneva Rd., Waterloo, 315/539-8848, www.fuzzyguppies.com), rents canoes, kayaks, and paddleboats by the hour or the day, and welcomes campers who want to pitch a tent. You can also rent time in the "human waterball," a huge, inflatable ball bobbing on the water. Climb inside, try to walk on water—and see if you can keep your balance.

After you've worked up an appetite paddling on the canal, nab a table at **RiverPark Grille** (1314 Waterloo-Geneva Rd., Waterloo, 315/539-0509, www. riverparkgrille.com, 11am-9pm Mon.-Sat), conveniently located next door to Fuzzy Guppies. Expect loaded nachos, chicken wings, and burgers.

AURORA

Halfway down Cayuga's expansive eastern shore is picture-perfect Aurora, with its houses laid out like beads on a string. Most date back to the mid-1800s; the village is on the National Register of Historic Places.

Called Deawendote, or Village of Constant Dawn, by the Cayuga, Aurora attracted its first European settlers in the late 1780s. Henry Wells founded Wells College here in 1868, and the school—a premier liberal arts college for women, which only went coed in 2005—remains a focal point of Main Street.

Also in Aurora is **MacKenzie-Childs** (3260 Rte. 90, 315/364-7123, www.mackenzie-childs. com, daily 10am-5pm), a classy home furnishings-design studio best known for its whimsical terra-cotta pottery. The studio employs about 100 craftspeople, who design everything from glassware to lamps, and is housed on a 19th-century estate with great views of the lake. Though the studio itself is no longer open for tours, MacKenzie-Childs hosts a visitors' center, where a video about the studio's craftsmanship is shown, and guests can take a free tour of the **Farmhouse,** a charming 15-room Victorian built in the 1800s. The tour features many MacKenzie-Childs products.

In the Tudor-style Aurora Free Library building, the charming, turn-of-the-century **Morgan Opera House** (Rte. 90 at Cherry Ave., 315/364-5437, www.morganoperahouse.org, May-Sept.) offers musical and dramatic events.

Accommodations and Food

One of the best options in the area is the lovely 1833 **Aurora Inn** (391 Main St., 315/364-8888, www.innsofaurora.com, $175-465). Inside, find 10 luxurious guest rooms furnished with antiques and Oriental rugs, a waterside restaurant (entrées $18-27) with views of the lake, and a cozy tavern with a fireplace and mahogany bar. On the menu of the highly-thought-of restaurant is refined American cuisine inspired by the seasons and fresh regional products paired perfectly with Finger Lakes wines.

E.B. Morgan House (431 Main St., 315/364-8888, $165-390) rents rooms individually or all seven for larger groups. When the entire house is rented, a private epicurean dinner option for up to 14 is available via Aurora Inn's Executive Chef Patrick Higgins.

For more casual dining, **Pumpkin Hill Bistro** (2051 Rte. 90, 315/364-7091, www.pumpkinhillbistro.com, lunch and dinner, hours vary seasonally, $9-14), housed in an 1820s hand-built dwelling, was transported to its current location in 2001. Burgers, panini sandwiches, and country favorites are enhanced by regional farm goods. Nightly specials and harvest brunches bring in a steady flow of locals.

ROMULUS

Midway down the west side of the lake lies Romulus, known for its vineyards and wineries. Two of the best wineries are only five miles apart. A very large operation, **Swedish Hill Winery** (4565 Rte. 414, 607/403-0029, www.swedishhill.com, tasting room year-round daily 9am-6pm) produces about 30,000 cases of 25 different kinds of wines a year. **Knapp Winery** (2770 County Rd. 128, 800/869-9271, www.knappwine.com, Apr.-Nov. daily 10am-5:30pm, Dec.-Mar. Mon.-Sat. 10:30am-5pm and Sun. 11:30am-5pm) is much smaller, but its wines are among the region's finest. Knapp's breezy **Vineyard Restaurant** (2770 County Rd. 128, 800/869-9271, Apr.-Nov. daily 11am-5pm, hours vary off-season, $13) emphasizes local produce.

OVID

Heading south of Romulus on Route 96, you'll come to the hamlet of Ovid, astride a small ridge surrounded by farmland. In the heart of the village stand three red-brick Greek Revival buildings known as the **Three Bears** because of the way they diminish progressively in size. "Papa Bear" was once the county courthouse; "Mama Bear," the village library; and "Baby Bear," the county jail. Today, the buildings house county offices.

Accommodations and Camping

Off Route 89 overlooking Cayuga Lake is **Sned-Acres Campground** (6590 S. Cayuga Lake Rd., 607/869-9787, www.sned-acres.com), a good place for families as it's equipped with a playground and miniature golf course.

Nearby is **Driftwood Inn B&B** (7401 Wyers Point Rd., Ovid, 607/532-4324, www.driftwoodny.com, $125-180), offering six guest rooms in the main house, and four cottages, which are available by the week. Out front is a 260-foot-long waterfront equipped with small boats and views of the lake.

TAUGHANNOCK FALLS

About 10 miles north of Ithaca thunder **Taughannock Falls,** a skinny but dazzling 215-foot-long stream of water flanked on either side by towering stone walls. Just 10,000

© JACK AIELLO/123RF

Taughannock Falls

years ago, the falls cascaded straight down into Cayuga Lake, but erosion has moved them almost a mile inland. Thirty feet higher than Niagara, Taughannock Falls are the highest straight falls east of the Rockies.

The falls are situated within the 783-acre **Taughannock Falls State Park** (2221 Taughannock Rd., 607/387-6739, camping reservations 800/456-2267, www.nysparks.com/parks/62, daily dawn-dusk, parking $7), which also offers lake swimming, fishing, boating, hiking, cabins, and a 76-site campground. Children will enjoy the park's imaginative playground, equipped with wooden towers and platforms. An overlook before the park gate offers a nice chance to see the falls without a commitment for those short on time. In July and August, free jazz, Latin, folk, and rock concerts take place weekly in the park.

Accommodations

Two lovely options in Trumansburg, close to Taughannock Falls, are the best bet for this area. The proximity to Ithaca (10 minutes) makes this peaceful alternate locale worthy of consideration for a base to explore that city.

The Halsey House (2057 Trumansburg Rd., 607/387-5428, www.halseyhouse.com, $209-289) sits at the entrance to the Taughannock Falls road and offers the perfect mix of romantic elegance and modern convenience (Wi-Fi, flatscreen TVs and a DVD collection, robes, complimentary snacks and drinks) in sumptuous bedded rooms with gorgeous upscale whirlpool bathrooms. Lovely innkeepers, a common area made cozier by a fireplace, and the included gourmet breakfast add to the experience.

Inn at Gothic Eves (112 E. Main, 607/387-6033, www.gothiceves.com, $189-259) is an 1855 inn nestled in the heart of the tiny village. This unique property offers a selection of rooms, most of which are named after wines, and a true farm-to-table breakfast using eggs, berries, and local cheeses, often harvested that very morning. A can't miss at this spot is a session in the outdoor wood-fired hot tub, which is included in the stay and is stoked by the innkeeper by appointment.

Ithaca

Idyllically situated at the southern edge of Cayuga Lake, Ithaca is all but surrounded by steep hills and gorges. Three powerful waterfalls plunge right through the heart of the city and give Ithaca the tagline that it's used for years: "Ithaca is gorges." The small, progressive university town has a population of just over 30,000—which nearly doubles in size whenever its two colleges, Cornell University and Ithaca College, are in session.

Ithaca was originally a Cayuga settlement that was destroyed during General Sullivan's ruthless 1779 campaign. The first white settlers arrived in 1788, but the town didn't really begin to grow until the opening of Cornell University in 1868.

For several years beginning in 1914, Ithaca was a center for the motion picture business. The Wharton Studios based itself here; *Exploits of Elaine,* starring Lionel Barrymore and Pearl White, and *Patria,* starring Irene Castle, were both filmed in Ithaca. The region's unpredictable weather proved less than ideal for moviemaking, however, and in 1920 the industry moved west.

Ithaca also claims to be the birthplace of the sundae, supposedly first concocted here in 1891. "As the story goes," writes Arch Merrill in *Slim Fingers Beckon,* "an Ithaca preacher came into C. C. Platt's drugstore, weary and sweating after the Sunday morning service. He asked the druggist to fix a dish of ice cream and pour some syrup on it...and thus another American institution was born."

Orientation

Downtown is small and compact. In its flat center lies **Ithaca Commons,** a pedestrian mall spread out along State Street. Perched on a steep hill to the east is Cornell University. The roller-coaster streets surrounding Cornell are known as **Collegetown.** On another hill to the south sits Ithaca College.

The best way to explore Ithaca and environs is by foot and car. Street parking is generally available, but there are also several municipal garages downtown.

SIGHTS
Ithaca Commons

The pedestrian-only Commons runs along State Street between Aurora and Cayuga Streets and along Tioga Street between Seneca and State Streets. Somewhat European in feel, it's filled with fountains, trees, flowers, and benches, and is flanked by shops and restaurants.

Most of the buildings along the Commons were constructed between the 1860s and the 1930s. Note the handsome Italianate building at **No. 158 E. State Street,** and the Art Deco storefront at **No. 152 E. State Street.** Just beyond the Commons, at **No. 101 W. State Street,** glows a 1947 neon sign of a cocky chanticleer.

The **Sagan Planet Walk** was built in memory of astronomer Carl Sagan, who was a resident of Ithaca. It starts at the "sun" on the Commons and continues on to visit nine "planets" along a 0.75-mile route leading to the ScienCenter Museum (www.sciencenter.org). Visitors who get their "Passport to the Solar System" stamped along the way earn a free visit to the museum.

Historic DeWitt Park

The oldest buildings in the city are located on or near DeWitt Park, a peaceful retreat at East Buffalo and North Cayuga Streets, one block north of DeWitt Mall. Many buildings in this National Historic District date to the early 1800s.

On the park's north side stands the 1817 **Old Courthouse** (121 E. Court St., 607/273-8284), thought to be the oldest Gothic Revival building in the state, and **First Presbyterian Church,** designed by James Renwick, the architect of St. Patrick's Cathedral in New York

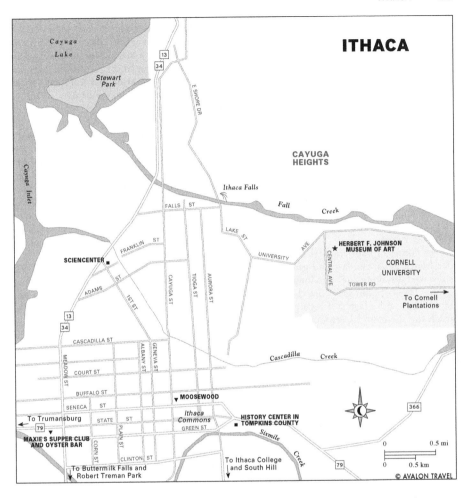

ITHACA

City. On the east side is the Romanesque **First Baptist Church,** built in 1890.

History Center in Tompkins County

Inside this large, renovated building you'll find the **History Center in Tompkins County** (401 E. State St., 607/273-8284, www.thehistory-center.net, Tues., Thurs., and Sat. 11am-5pm, free), run by the DeWitt Historical Society. The society owns an impressive collection of over 20,000 objects, 3,000 books, and 100,000 photographs.

Permanent displays show the city's beginnings, its industries, and its surprising film history. Temporary exhibits have focused on such subjects as folk arts, alternative medicine, Italian immigrants, and Finnish-American saunas.

The ScienCenter

The hands-on **ScienCenter** (601 1st St.,

607/272-0600, www.sciencenter.org, Tues.-Sat. 10am-5pm, Sun. noon-5pm, adults $8, seniors $7, children 3-17 $6) primarily appeals to young ones, but adults can learn something here as well. Pre-schoolers can play in the Curiosity Corner, which has a water table and craft area, while older kids will probably head to the Animal Room or space exhibits. The museum has an extensive set of activities outside, too. In addition to mini-golf, there's a "create your own waterfall" activity, a geometry climber, the world's only Kevlar cable suspension bridge, a giant lever, whisper dishes, and a "bubble-ology" section in outdoor Emerson Science Park.

Ithaca Falls

At the corner of Falls and Lake Streets thunder Ithaca Falls, the last and greatest of the six waterfalls along the mile-long Fall Creek gorge. These "pulpit falls" are closely-spaced rapids created by layers of resistant rock. To reach the site from Ithaca Commons—about a 20-minute walk—head north along Cayuga Street to Falls Street and turn right. To one side is a small grassy park and a wooded path that leads to a popular fishing hole.

Cornell University

Cornell University, built around a long, lush green lined with ivy-covered buildings, sits high on a hill overlooking downtown Ithaca. The views from here are especially fine at twilight, when Cayuga's waters glow with the setting sun and the gorges begin a slow fade into black.

Cornell was founded in 1865 by Ezra Cornell and Andrew D. White, who vowed to establish an "institution where any person can find instruction in any study." In so doing, they challenged a number of long-standing mores. Their university was one of the first to be non-sectarian; to offer instruction to all qualified applicants, regardless of sex, race, or class; and to feature courses in everything from agriculture to the classics.

Traffic and information booths are located at each entrance to the central campus. Except in

a few metered areas, parking is by permit only; purchase a permit at the traffic booths. Visitors to the Herbert F. Johnson Museum can park in metered spaces out front. To tour the campus, contact the **Information and Referral Center** (Day Hall, Tower Rd. and East Ave., 607/254-4636, www.cornell.edu).

HERBERT F. JOHNSON MUSEUM OF ART

At the northern end of the Cornell campus is the **Herbert F. Johnson Museum of Art** (114 Central Ave., 607/255-6464, www.museum.cornell.edu, Tues.-Sun. 10am-5pm, free), housed in a striking modern building designed by I. M. Pei. The museum features especially strong collections of Asian and contemporary art but is also a teaching museum, containing a little bit of almost everything.

The Asian collection is situated on the 5th floor, where big picture windows open out onto 360-degree views of Cayuga Lake and the surrounding countryside. Among the many exquisite objects on display are funerary urns from the T'ang dynasty, silk paintings from 19th-century Japan, and bronze Buddhas from 15th-century Thailand.

WILDER BRAIN COLLECTION

Those interested in the odd and macabre will want to step into Cornell's Uris Hall (East Ave. and Tower Rd.) and ride an elevator up to the second floor. In a small case to the rear of the building are eight of the surviving stars of the Burt Green Wilder brain collection, which once numbered about 600 floating specimens.

Wilder, a former Civil War surgeon, was Cornell's first zoologist. He began assembling his collection in the late 1800s in the hopes of proving the size and shape of a person's brain were related to his or her race, sex, intelligence, and personality. Alas, his studies only disproved his theories, and in 1911 he rocked the scientific world by declaring that there was no difference between the brains of black and white men.

The pickled collection includes the extraordinarily large brain of criminal Edward Howard Ruloff, who was hanged in Binghamton on

May 18, 1871. Ruloff allegedly killed his wife and daughter and was convicted of killing three men. He was also highly intelligent, and had published several scholarly papers despite his lack of formal education.

Burt Green Wilder's brain is also in the collection. Considerably smaller than Ruloff's, it sits yellowing in viscous formaldehyde. The creator has joined his creation.

Cornell Plantations

Just north of the Cornell campus, 2,800-acre **Cornell Plantations** (124 Comstock Knoll Dr., 607/255-2400, www.cornellplantations. org, daily dawn-dusk, free) is an oasis of green. It encompasses a botanical garden, nature preserve, and arboretum, with specialty gardens devoted to everything from wildflowers to poisonous plants. Walkable nature trails wind through the Fall Creek gorge. Pick up maps in the **visitors' center** (Tues.-Sat. 10am-4pm).

Sapsucker Woods Bird Sanctuary

At the eastern edge of the city lies a world-class center for the study, appreciation, and conservation of birds. Not everything is open to the public, but key attractions include 4.2 miles of trails through the Sapsucker Woods Sanctuary and Stuart Observatory, which overlooks a waterfowl pond and bird-feeding garden.

The 230-acre Sapsucker Woods were named by bird artist Louis Agassiz Fuertes in 1901 after he spotted a pair of yellow-bellied sapsuckers—unusual for the region—nesting in the area. Sapsuckers continue to breed here each year. Near the woods you'll find a **visitors' center** (159 Sapsucker Woods Rd., 800/843-2473, www.birds.cornell.edu, Mon.-Thurs. 8am-5pm, Fri. 8am-4pm, Sat. 9:30am-4pm, Sun. 11am-4pm, free), where you can pick up maps and view paintings by Agassiz Fuertes.

Buttermilk Falls State Park

Just south of downtown is **Buttermilk Falls State Park** (Rte. 13, 607/273-5761, camping reservations 800/456-2267, www.nysparks.com/parks/151, May-Nov. daily dawn-dusk, parking $7), plummeting more than 500 feet past 10 waterfalls, churning rapids, sculptured pools, and raggedy cliffs. Alongside the falls runs a trail leading up to spire-like Pinnacle Rock and Treman Lake. At the base of the falls are a natural swimming hole, ball fields, and a campground.

Robert H. Treman State Park

Robert H. Treman State Park (105 Enfield Falls Rd., 607/273-3440, camping reservations 800/456-2267, Apr.-Nov. daily dawn-dusk, parking $7), five miles south of Ithaca, is 1,025 acres of wild and rugged beauty. Near the entrance is Enfield Glen, a forested gorge traversed by a stone pathway and steps. The steps lead to 115-foot-high Lucifer Falls and a vista stretching 1.5 miles down into a deep glen threaded by the Gorge Trail. A three-story 1839 gristmill, a natural swimming pool, and a campground are also on the grounds.

ENTERTAINMENT AND EVENTS

Cornell's **Schwartz Center for the Performing Arts** (430 College Ave., 607/254-2787) stages 6-12 plays September-May, along with the Cornell Dance Series and numerous guest performances. Professional regional theater is staged by acclaimed **Hangar Theatre** (801 Taughannock Blvd., 607/273-8588, www.hangartheatre.org, June-Aug.). The **Kitchen Theatre** (417 W. State St., 607/272-0403 or 607/272-0570, www.kitchentheatre.org) presents contemporary theater year-round in an intimate space.

Among the groups performing regularly in the city is **Cayuga Chamber Orchestra** (171 E. State St., 607/273-8981, www.ccoithaca.org), the official orchestra of Ithaca. **Ithaca Ballet** (607/277-1967, www.ithacaballet.org) performs both classical and contemporary works.

Good club listings can be found in *Ithaca Times* (www.ithaca.com), a free alternative news weekly.

Many of the local galleries participate in the monthly **First Friday Gallery Night** (www.gallerynightithaca.wordpress.com), a free event that takes place from 5pm-8pm. Galleries and shops stay open late, inviting visitors to browse art and enjoy special exhibits and live performances.

SHOPPING

One block north of the Commons, at the corner of Seneca and Cayuga Streets, is **DeWitt Mall** (215 N. Cayuga St.). This former school building now contains about 20 shops, galleries, and restaurants. Among the galleries is **Sola Art Gallery** (607/272-6552, www.solagallery.com, Mon.-Sat. 10:30am-5:30pm), which specializes in Japanese woodblock prints.

Handwork (102 W. State St., 607/273-9400, www.handwork.coop, Mon.-Wed. and Sat. 10am-6pm, Thurs.-Fri. 10am-8pm, Sun. noon-5pm) is a craft co-op showcasing the work of over 30 local craftspeople. Here, you can find jewelry, clocks, glass, ceramic, fiber, and leatherwork, and home accessories, such as handmade wooden cutting boards.

As its name suggests, **Ithacamade** (430 W. State St., 607/272-1396, www.ithacamade.com) is a gallery specializing in arts and crafts made by Ithacans. In addition to jewelry, pottery, and decorative arts, Ithacamade also has soap and snacks like macarons and biscotti for sale.

SPORTS AND RECREATION

Circle Greenway is a 10-mile self-guided walk or bike ride that leads to many of Ithaca's foremost natural and urban attractions, including gorges, the waterfront, Cornell, and the Commons. A free map can be picked up at **Ithaca/Tompkins County Convention and Visitors Bureau** (904 E. Shore Dr., 607/272-1313, www.visitithaca.com).

Cayuga Lake Cruises (708 W. Buffalo St., 607/256-0898, www.cayugalakecruises.com) offers dinner, lunch, brunch, and cocktail cruises aboard the M/V *Columbia*. **Ithaca Boat Tours** (607/697-0166, www.ithacaboattours.com, $12 adults, $10 seniors and students, $8 children 5-12) offers narrated one-hour tours of the lake that depart from the Farmers Market pier at 11am and 12:30pm Saturdays

and Sundays, May 1 to October 31. Two-hour tours (adults $18, seniors and students $16, children 5-12 $12) are offered on Tuesdays, Wednesdays, and Fridays, and ecotours (adults $18, seniors and students $16, children 5-12 $12) are scheduled for Thursdays and Sundays.

ACCOMMODATIONS

As the teaching hotel of Cornell's School of Hotel Administration, the **Statler Hotel** (130 Statler Dr., 607/257-2500, www.statlerhotel.cornell.edu, $165-680) is Ithaca's hotel of choice for visiting parents, academics, and travelers. The hotel features 153 guest rooms, two restaurants, and a café and lounge; guests have access to most of Cornell's facilities, including the gym, pool, tennis courts, and golf course.

The very unique **Log Country Inn B&B** (4 Larue Rd., 607/589-4771, www.logtv.com/inn, $70-150) may sound rustic but it features soaring cathedral ceilings, fireplaces, a sauna, and 11 guest rooms, some with whirlpool tubs. Each room is named for a particular country or region of the world. A trip to the website is suggested to handpick a vibe of choice. Next door is a 7,000-acre forest, perfect for hiking and cross-country skiing. Some rooms share baths.

City Lights Inn (1319 Mecklenburg Rd., 607/227-3003, www.theinnatcitylights.com, $135-155) offers warm service, roomy suites (some with full kitchen and wood stove), and cozy bedrooms, all with private bath and modern amenities. The garden is a nice place to relax or to enjoy Ithaca's fireworks displays on holidays.

The picturesque **William Henry Miller Inn** (303 N. Aurora St., 607/256-4553, www.millerinn.com, $155-185) is an 1880 home and carriage house filled with stained glass and carved wood details. It has high-ceilinged rooms with private baths (some with whirlpool tubs) and modern amenities, warm service, evening dessert with coffee, and gourmet breakfast with offerings such as poached eggs with sun dried tomato hollandaise or crème brulee French toast.

For more bed-and-breakfast suggestions, contact the **Ithaca/Tompkins County**

Convention and Visitors Bureau (904 E. Shore Dr., 607/272-1313, www.visitithaca.com) or **Bed & Breakfast of Greater Ithaca** (800/806-4406, www.bbithaca.com). You can also check room availability by visiting the visitors bureau's website www.visitithaca.com.

FOOD

A number of casual eateries are located along Ithaca Commons. The 100 block of Aurora Street just off the Commons has one restaurant after another.

The cooperatively owned **🅲 Moosewood Restaurant** (215 N. Cayuga St., DeWitt Mall, 607/273-9610, www.moosewoodcooks.com, Sun. 5:30pm-8:30pm, Mon.-Thurs. 11:30am-3pm and 5:30pm-8:30pm, Fri.-Sat. 11:30am-3pm and 5:30pm-9pm, $18) opened in 1973 and has been serving creative vegetarian cuisine ever since. It has made a name for itself worldwide for its best-selling cookbooks and natural foods. An outdoor dining area is open in summer.

Also serving contemporary American cuisine, as well as seafood, **BoatYard Grill** (525 Taughannock Blvd., 607/256-2628, www.boatyardgrill.com, daily lunch and dinner, $17) overlooks the waterfront.

Just a Taste (116 N. Aurora St., 607/277-9463, www.just-a-taste.com, Sun.-Thurs. 5:30pm-10pm, Fri.-Sat. 5:30pm-11pm, average tapa $8-10), Ithaca's wine and tapas bar, serves 50 wines by the glass and a menu inspired by Spain's small, sharable dishes, called tapas. Outside is a lovely garden. A couple blocks north, **Madeline's** (215 E. State St., 607/277-2253, www.madelines-restaurant.com, Sun.-Wed. 5pm-10pm, Thurs.-Sat. 5pm-11pm, $20) offers excellent "Euro-Asian fusion."

Hot spot **Maxie's Supper Club and Oyster Bar** (635 W. State St., 607/272-4136, www.maxies.com, daily 4pm-11pm, $14), evokes New Orleans with its decor, attitude, and, of course, spicy Cajun cuisine and stick-to-your-ribs Southern soul food. Everything is homemade at this family-run affair.

Seneca Lake

At just over 36 miles long and 618 feet deep, Seneca Lake is the deepest lake in New York State. It seldom freezes over and is renowned for its superb lake-trout fishing. Given to sudden, capricious gusts of wind, it's the most mysterious of the Finger Lakes.

Ever since the days of the Native Americans, area residents have reported strange, dull rumblings coming from Seneca's depths. The sounds are usually heard at dusk in the late summer or early fall and are most distinct midway down the lake. Native Americans believed the rumblings were the voice of an angry god. Early settlers considered them omens of disaster. Science attributes them to the popping of natural gas released from rock rifts at the bottom of the lake.

Whatever the cause, the dull rumbles—a sound much like gunfire—may have had some portent, for during World War II, a

huge munitions depot was built along Seneca's eastern shore. The 10,500+-acre Seneca Army Depot remains, though it ceased operations in the 1990s and was shuttered in 2000. A herd of snow-white deer roam the grounds and can best be seen from Route 96A at dawn and dusk.

At the northern end of Seneca Lake lies Geneva, a historic town whose South Main Street has been called "the most beautiful street in America." At the southern end is Watkins Glen, a village known for the birth of American road racing. It's also home to a rugged, 700-foot-deep gorge that's been turned into a natural theme park.

GENEVA

One of the larger towns in the region, Geneva is home to about 13,200 residents. Though overall a nondescript place, elegant South Main

Street, lined with leafy trees, stately homes, and Hobart and William Smith Colleges, runs through its center.

Geneva was once a major Seneca settlement known as Kanadesaga. During the French and Indian War, the British erected a fort here from which they and the Seneca conducted murderous raids, only to be massacred themselves during the 1779 Sullivan campaign.

Soon after the Revolution, European settlers began to arrive. A visionary land agent laid out the town along a broad Main Street and a public green. This gave the place an air of dignity, which, during the 1800s, attracted an unusually large number of retired ministers and spinsters. Geneva soon earned the nickname "The Saints' Retreat and Old Maids' Paradise."

In 1847, the Medical College of Geneva College (now Hobart) received an application of admission from Elizabeth Blackwell of Philadelphia. The students and deans, assuming it to be a joke, laughingly voted to admit her. A few weeks later, to everyone's amazement, Ms. Blackwell arrived, and in 1849, she graduated—the first woman ever granted a medical diploma in America.

Rose Hill Mansion

Three miles east of downtown lies Geneva's foremost visitor attraction, the 1839 **Rose Hill Mansion** (3373 Rte. 96A, 315/789-3848, May 1-June and Sept.-Oct. 31 Mon.-Fri. 9:30am-4:30pm and Sat. 1:30pm-4:30pm, Nov. 1-Apr. 30 Tues.-Fri. 9:30am-4:30pm and Sat. 1:30pm-4:30pm, July-Aug. Mon.-Fri. 9:30am-4:30pm and Sat.-Sun. 1:30pm-4:30pm, adults $7, seniors $6, children 10-18 $4, children under 10 free), built in the Greek Revival style with six Ionic columns out front. The mansion was once home to Robert Swan, an innovative farmer who installed the country's first large-scale drainage system. Tours of the house take visitors past a fine collection of Empire-style furnishings. Next door is the former carriage house; out front, the green lawn slopes down to Seneca Lake.

Prouty-Chew House

Built in the Federal style in 1829 by a Geneva attorney, the **Prouty-Chew House** (543 S. Main St., 315/789-5151, www.genevahistoricalsociety.com, hours vary seasonally, free) was enlarged several times in the 1850s and 1870s, which accounts for its eclectic look. It's now home to the Geneva Historical Society, which showcases changing exhibits on local history and art.

Wine Tasting

The regional wine passport program offers the best deal for tastings at wineries throughout the area.

Three Brothers Wineries & Estates (623 Lerch Rd., Geneva, 315/585-4432, www.3brotherswinery.com, open 10am-5pm) offers three distinct wineries and one microbrewery. The tasting room of each has its own unique vibe. Stony Lonesome Estates is all hard wood and class, while Passion Feet is sexy with velvet accents, and Bagg Dare is down-home, kick-back casual.

Five bucks gets you five tastings at **Zugibe Vineyards** (4248 East Lake Rd., Geneva, 315/585-6402, www.zugibevineyards.com, 11am-5pm daily). Take a seat on the porch and enjoy the unobstructed views of Seneca Lake while you sip your way through Cab Sauvs, Gruner Veltliners, and the lesser-known Lembergers.

The tasting room at **Ventosa Vineyards** (3440 Rte. 96A, Geneva, 315/719-0000, www.ventosavineyards.com, 11am-5pm Mon.-Thurs. and Sat., 10am-9pm Fri., noon-5pm Sun.) opens up to beautiful lake views, but it's popular among oenophiles in part because it's open late on Friday, when it also hosts live music. The Italian cafe just off the tasting room serves light bites (11am-5pm daily).

Accommodations and Food

For dockside dining, try **The Crow's Nest** (415 Boody's Hill Rd., 315/781-0600, www.thecrowsnestrestaurant.com, daily lunch and dinner, $14). Sandwiches, salads, seafood, and beef are on the menu here.

Red Dove Tavern (30 Castle St., 315/781-2020, www.reddovetavern.com, hours vary seasonally, $25) features American fare comprised of local ingredients. Entrées change weekly based on what's in season.

The extravagant, Romanesque **Belhurst Castle** (4069 West Lake Rd., 315/781-0201, www.belhurst.com, $110-395 d, with breakfast) took 50 workers toiling six days a week for four years to complete. Finished in 1889, it features everything from turrets to stained-glass windows. Inside is **Edgar's** (average lunch entrée $9, average dinner entrée $24), an upscale restaurant serving continental fare for both lunch and dinner, and **Stonecutters** (daily lunch and dinner, $12), which offers a tavern-style menu. Fourteen modern guest rooms vary greatly in size and price. An on-site spa-salon pampers guests and a winery offers tours and tastings. Out front are formal gardens and a lakefront beach. Also operated by Belhurst Castle are the lovely Georgian **White Springs Manor** (315/781-0201, www.belhurst.com, $110-395 d) and **Vinifera Inn** (315/781-0201, www.belhurst.com, $110-395 d).

The luxurious, all-suite **Geneva-on-the-Lake** (1001 Lochland Rd., 315/789-7190, www.genevaonthelake.com, $210-550, with continental breakfast) is especially popular among honeymooners. The property centers around a 1911 mansion built in the style of a 16th-century Italian villa. Each suite differs from the next. Outside are 10 acres of formal gardens. The **dining room** (average dinner entrée $36), open to the public for lunch and dinner, serves continental fare using fresh local produce.

Stivers Seneca Marina (401 Boody's Hill Rd., Waterloo, 315/789-0377, www.stiversseneca marine.com) offers a unique lodging alternative. You can remain docked at Stivers' own marina, which has a very good on-site restaurant, or choose to motor slowly along the canal on a multi-day itinerary in the houseboat, which has four bedrooms, a full kitchen, two full baths, a living room, a hot tub, and a slide. Weekly rentals are $4,550.

DETOUR TO SODUS POINT

Sodus Point, which overlooks Lake Ontario, is worth a 30-mile detour north of Geneva on Route 14. The village boasts gorgeous views and an inviting public beach.

Sodus Bay Lighthouse Museum

The handsome 1870 **Sodus Bay Lighthouse Museum** (7606 N. Ontario St., 315/483-4936, www.soduspointlighthouse.org, May 1-Oct. 31 Tues.-Sun. 10am-5pm, $4 adults, children 8-17 $2) in a three-story stone block structure is dedicated to maritime and regional history. The lighthouse tower, about 50 feet high, is open to visitors who can climb the 52 circular steps into the lens room. From there, it's a gorgeous view of the Lake Ontario shoreline.

Chimney Bluffs State Park

Located on the eastern side of Sodus Bay, the **Chimney Bluffs** rise 150 feet above the lake like some giant confectionery delight. All pinnacles, spires, and peaks, they're part of a glacier-created drumlin that has been eroded, carved, and shaped by water, wind, and snow. Atop some of the pinnacles sit lone trees; below them extends a stony beach. Scuba divers exiting Lake Ontario are another unexpected sight on the beach.

Dozens of other drumlins (minus the pinnacles and peaks) can be found throughout this part of the Lake Ontario region. The only other places to view drumlins in North America are the areas bordering Lake Superior in Minnesota.

Chimney Bluffs and its beach form part of the undeveloped **Chimney Bluffs State Park** (7700 Garner Rd., Wolcott, www.nysparks.com/parks/43, daily dawn-dusk, free).

Alasa Farms and Crackerbox Palace

On your way to and from Sodus Point, you'll pass through farm country, heavy with rich black soil. Apples, cherries, and peaches thrive in this climate, as do corn, wheat, potatoes, onions, and lettuce.

Off Route 14 just south of Sodus Point lies

Alasa Farms. Once a 1,400-acre Shaker religious community, the site passed into private hands in the 1800s. Throughout the 1920s and 1930s, the farm raised everything from shorthorn cattle and hackney ponies to timberland and orchards. Today, it's home to **Crackerbox Palace** (6450 Shaker Rd., Alton, 315/483-2493, www.crackerboxpalace.org, Sat. 10am-3pm and by appt., $5 per person), a nonprofit farm haven that rescues and cares for abused and abandoned animals. Tours are available on Saturdays and by appointment.

Events
One of the region's foremost events is **Sterling Renaissance Festival** (800/879-4446, www.sterlingfestival.com), held in Sterling, near Fair Haven, about 25 miles west of Sodus Point. For seven weekends in July and August, the fest celebrates the Middle Ages with music, jousting, outdoor theater, crafts, and food.

Accommodations
Several lovely B&Bs are in the heart of Sodus Point.

Carriage House Inn (8375 Wickham Blvd., 315/483-2100, www.Carriage-House-Inn.com), an 1870s Victorian B&B, offers four guest rooms, all with king beds and private baths. Guests can walk along the beach for about a half mile to reach the Sodus Bay Lighthouse Museum.

Maxwell Creek Inn B&B (7563 Lake Rd., 315/483-2222, www.maxwellcreekinn-bnb.com, $135-159) is an historic 1846 cobblestone house located on the Seaway Trail. It has five guest rooms in the main building, as well as a private cobblestone cottage that has two efficiency suites, each with a kitchenette and private bath.

Silver Waters B&B (8420 Bay St., 315/483-8098, www.silver-waters.com, $85-139) is an historic inn in the center of Sodus Point Village, featuring four guest rooms, each with a private bath. From here, it's a quick walk to the Sodus Bay Lighthouse Museum.

Situated on 5.4 acres with a combination of woods and 340 feet of lakeshore, **The Cliffs at Sodus Point** (7961 Lake Rd., 315/483-4309. www.thecliffsatsoduspoint.com, $135-155) features five guest rooms with private baths. The B&B also has a gift shop on-site, where you can buy hand-painted wine glasses and handmade wine stoppers and jewelry.

◖ WINE ROUTES
Heading south from Geneva on either side of Seneca Lake, you'll find a series of vineyards worth a visit. Route 14 runs south along the western shore of the lake, while Routes 96A and 414 run along the eastern shore. Both routes offer excellent wineries and scenic views, both from the vineyards and tasting rooms, as well as the roads you take to reach them. If you don't have time for both routes, choose the Route 14 wineries, which will allow the opportunity to pass through Watkins Glen and catch a view of its spectacular falls and gorges.

South on Route 14
From Geneva, Route 14 heads south along the western shore of Seneca Lake past two excellent wineries. **Fox Run Vineyards** (670 Rte. 14, Penn Yan, 315/536-4616, www.foxrunvineyards.com, Mon.-Sat. 10am-6pm, Sun. 11am-6pm) is housed in an 1860s dairy barn with sweeping views of the lake. Fox Run produces more than 90 wines, including ports. **Anthony Road Wine Company** (1020 Anthony Rd., Penn Yan, 800/559-2182, www.anthonyroadwine.com, Mon.-Sat. 10am-5pm, Sun. noon-5pm) produces a variety of reds, whites, and dessert wines.

More good wineries are clustered near the lake's southern end. Among them is **Hermann J. Wiemer Vineyard** (3962 Rte. 14, Dundee, 607/243-7971, www.wiemer.com, Mon.-Sat. 10am-5pm, Sun. 11am-5pm), founded by a foremost viticulturist who came from a family that made wine in Germany for more than 300 years. The winery is best known for its Rieslings.

About five miles farther south is **Glenora Wine Cellars** (5435 Rte. 14, Dundee, 607/243-9500, www.glenora.com, hours vary seasonally). Established in 1977, Glenora is best

THE VINEYARDS OF THE FINGER LAKES

The hills of the Finger Lakes, covered with vineyards, glow pale green in spring, brilliant green in summer, and red-brown-purple in fall. The conditions for ideal grape-growing were set into motion tens of thousands of years ago when retreating glaciers deposited a layer of topsoil on shale beds above the lakes, which create a microclimate that moderates the region's temperatures.

It wasn't until the 19th century, though, that winemaking began to take root in the Finger Lakes. A minister whose intent was to make sacramental wine planted some vines near Hammondsport in 1829. The yield was successful; soon, neighbors planted their own vines, and vineyards ringed the village. In 1860, 13 Hammondsport businesspeople banded together to form the country's first commercial winery: Pleasant Valley Wine Company. Dozens of other entrepreneurs soon followed suit.

For many years, the Finger Lakes vineyards produced only native American Concord, Delaware, and Niagara grapes, used in the production of ho-hum sweet and table wines. About 25 years ago, however, several viticulturists began experimenting with the more complex European Vinifera grape. Today, a staggering number and variety of wines are produced here, including cabernet franc, cabernet sauvignon, Cayuga white, chardonnay, gewurztraminer, lemberger, merlot, pinot gris, pinot noir, Riesling, seyval blanc, vidal blanc, traminette, and both ice and iced wines.

Called "Napa Valley of the East," the Finger Lakes region currently boasts more than 100 wineries, most of which overlook Canandaigua, Cayuga, Keuka, or Seneca Lakes. Each lake has its own wine trail program, which publishes free maps and brochures and manages a "passport" program offering tasting discounts. Information about the wine trails can be found on the official Finger Lakes Wine Country website (www.fingerlakeswinecountry.com).

Most wineries are open daily 10am-5pm, year-round. Smaller wineries may close their tasting rooms in winter or reduce days or hours; call first. Tastings typically cost $2-5, an amount that's usually applied against your bill if you buy any bottles.

For a complete list of wineries, contact **Finger Lakes Wine Country** (607-936-0706, www.fingerlakeswinecountry.com).

---

known for sparkling wines. Its tasting room offers views of vineyards and of Seneca Lake. The winery also runs **Inn at Glenora Wine Cellars** (5435 Rte. 14, 607/243-9500, www.glenora. com, $160-255), whose spacious rooms feature picture windows overlooking vineyards, as well as private balconies or patios. Whether you're a guest at the inn or just passing through, you can dine at the winery's restaurant, **Veraisons** (5435 Rte. 14, 607/243-9500, www.glenora. com, average entrées $28), where the specialty is "regional fusion" fare. In summer months, enjoy your meal on the restaurant's outdoor dining patio.

Fulkerson Winery (5576 Rte. 14, Dundee, 607/243-7883, www.fulkersonwinery.com, daily 10am-5pm) has a large, light-filled tasting room, where staff will happily pour sips for you while sharing the Fulkerson family's fascinating history. Now in their seventh generation of farming, the Fulkersons trace their ancestry all the way back to the family's original farm...on New York City's Wall Street. Today, operations are firmly rooted in the Finger Lakes, where visitors can tour vineyards on foot or horseback or take a free winemaking class on weekends. An adjacent house owned by the family, and built in 1856, can be rented out by families or small groups. With four bedrooms, an enormous and fully-equipped kitchen, large dining room and living room, and 2.5 bathrooms (plus a washer and dryer), the house is a fantastic home base for exploring the region.

South on Routes 96A and 414

From Geneva, Route 96A heads south along the eastern shore of Seneca Lake. About 10 miles down is the 1,852-acre **Sampson**

© FRANCISCO COLLAZO

grounds of the Glenora Wine Cellars

State Park (6096 Rte. 96A, 315/585-6392, camping reservations 800/456-2267, www.nysparks.com/parks/154, parking $7), once a naval station where thousands of service members trained during World War II. Today, the park is equipped with a marina, swimming beach, bathhouses, picnic area, playground, and 245-site campground. South of Willard, Route 96A veers inland to Ovid, in the Cayuga Lake area, where it meets Route 414. Continue south on Route 414 to more small villages and a cluster of vineyards and wineries.

You'll find several wineries around the village of Lodi. Among them is **Lamoreaux Landing Wine Cellars** (9224 Rte. 414, 607/582-6011, www.lamoreauxwine.com, Mon.-Sat. 10am-5pm, Sun. noon-5pm), housed in a Greek Revival building with great views of the lake. Lamoreaux produces everything from chardonnay to pinot noir.

A few more miles down the road sprawls **Wagner Vineyards** (9322 Rte. 414, 607/582-6450, www.wagnervineyards.com, daily 10am-5pm). Its hub is a weathered octagonal building overlooking the lake. Established in 1979, Wagner produces over 30 different wines. On the premises is a microbrewery (www.wagnerbrewing.com) and **Ginny Lee Cafe** (607/582-6574, www.theginnylee.com), open for lunch and Sunday brunch only. On summer Friday nights, Wagner hosts "Fridays on the Deck," a hugely popular live music series. Locals crowd the deck and the generous-size lawn to eat, drink, and dance.

WATKINS GLEN AND VICINITY

Watkins Glen, named for the astonishing gorge that cuts through its center, sits at the southern tip of Seneca Lake. The glen, which is a popular state park, is easily accessible from the main roadway, where you'll find many family-friendly restaurants and lots of shops.

From 1948-1952, the main street of Watkins Glen and the steep roads surrounding it were the speedway of the American Grand Prix.

© FRANCISCO COLLAZO

the distinctive octagonal building at Wagner Vineyards

During the races, as many as 75,000 spectators descended on the village, whose year-round population was under 3,000. Today, world-class auto races take place at the **Watkins Glen International** (2790 Rte. 16, 607/535-2486, www.theglen.com), a racetrack four miles south of Watkins Glen. The **Grand Prix Festival** (www.grandprixfestival.com) in early September commemorates the town's legacy, re-enacting the 1948 American Grand Prix, complete with vintage vehicles.

◖ Watkins Glen State Park
Created some 12,000 years ago during the last Ice Age, **Watkins Glen State Park** (off Rte. 14, 607/535-4511, www.nysparks.com/parks/142, daily 8am-dusk, parking $8) is a wild and raggedy gorge flanked by high cliffs and strange, sculpted rock formations. Glen Creek—which drops some 700 feet in two miles over rapids, cascades, and 19 waterfalls—rushes through its center.

Alongside the gorge runs the 1.5-mile Gorge Trail, made up of 832 stone steps, stone paths, and numerous bridges. The trail leads past tunnels, caves, and a natural stone bridge, all carved out of the sedimentary rock by Glen Creek. If you hike the trail on a fine summer's day, you'll have lots of company, but the gorge inspires awe nonetheless.

The park also offers **campgrounds** (reservations 800/456-2267).

Montour Falls
Route 14 leads south of Watkins Glen through narrow, winding Pine Valley to Montour Falls, a small industrial community surrounded by seven glens. In the middle of town is **Shequaga Falls,** plunging downward 165 feet into a deep pool. The falls are illuminated at night; near the top is a pedestrian bridge.

Along Genesee and Main Streets you'll find a handsome **National Historic District,** known as the Glorious "T" District, composed of 24 brick buildings dating back to the 1850s. Among them is Memorial Library with its Tiffany windows and the Greek Revival Village Hall.

© FRANCISCO COLLAZO

a marina on Seneca Lake, in Watkins Glen

Sports and Recreation

World-class auto racing takes place April-October at **Watkins Glen International** (2790 Rte. 16, 607/535-2486, www.theglen.com). Ticket prices vary by event.

From early May until late October, 50-minute cruises of Seneca Lake are offered every hour on the hour by **Captain Bill's Seneca Lake Cruises** (1 N. Franklin St., 607/535-4541, www.senecaharborstation.com). Captain Bill also runs dinner cruises.

Another way to experience the lake by boat is to go on an excursion on the *True Love* (Dock at Village Pier, 607/535-5253, www.schoonerexcursions.com, $29-49 per person), a restored 1926 schooner made famous by its role in the movie *High Society*, which featured Louis Armstrong, Bing Crosby, Grace Kelly, and Frank Sinatra. Morning, mid-day, afternoon, and sunset sails are offered early May-late October. Charter sails are also available.

If you're looking for a more active way to experience Watkins Glen, **Summit to Stream Adventures** (3192 Abrams Rd., 607/535-2701, www.summittostream.com) offers chartered fly-fishing and steelhead/salmon fishing excursions, as well as guided kayak and canoe trips and gear rentals.

Accommodations

One of the more idiosyncratic lodging options in the area is **Seneca Lodge** (3600 Rte. 419, 607/535-2014, www.senecalodge.com, $75-99). A favorite haunt of bow hunters and race mechanics, the lodge centers around a restaurant and tavern whose back wall, bristled with arrows, looks like the hide of a porcupine and from whose ceiling hang NASCAR champs' tires and Formula One laurel wreaths. Accommodations consist of basic camp-style A-frames, cabins, and motel rooms.

Magnolia Place Bed and Breakfast (5240 Rte. 414, Hector, 607/546-5338, www.magnoliawelcome.com, $140-190), an 1830 farmhouse located about seven miles outside of Watkins Glen, offers eight suites overlooking Seneca Lake. Innkeepers talented in the culinary arts host wine tastings and create hot

© FRANCISCO COLLAZO

Watkins Glen State Park

breakfasts of "Dutch babies" with cinnamon biscuits, or corn fritters with house-smoked salmon, crème fraiche, and a poached egg. They also provide homemade evening sweets and dinner or hors d'oeuvres on request.

Watkins Glen Harbor Hotel (16 N. Franklin St., 607/535-6116, www.watkinsglenharborhotel.com, $159-339), situated on Seneca Lake's waterfront, is a newer hotel that's a favorite of NASCAR drivers and their entourages during race weekends. Large, airy rooms feature lush bedding and spa-style baths. Lake-facing rooms, which have balconies, are particularly coveted. The hotel's dining options include alfresco in season, a classic country club sports bar, and Blue Pointe Grille restaurant.

Food

Classic Chef's (2250 Rte. 14, Montour Falls, 607/535-9975, Sun.-Thurs. 6:30am-8:30pm, Fri.-Sat. 6:30am-9:30pm) is a classic American eatery, now in its sixth decade. Come here for tasty pancakes or grilled cheese sandwiches.

Wildflower Café & the Crooked Rooster Brewpub (223-301 N. Franklin St., 607/535-9797, www.roosterfishbrewing.com, $14) offers tasty organic fare, from creative sandwiches to hearty meals and fresh, house-made pizzas. Roosterfish ales are another big draw.

Chef-owned **Dano's Heuriger on Seneca** (9564 Rte. 414, Lodi, 607/582-7555, www.danosonseneca.com, $12), with glass-walled lakeside dining, combines the tastes of a traditional Viennese wine restaurant with the Finger Lake's best vintages. Charcuterie and schnitzel, authentic Viennese casual ordering style and Austrian traditions, like a festival celebrating the harvest with newly fermented wine, add to the charm. A chef's table is available on request for parties of six or more.

Just west of the village, you'll find **Castel Grisch Estate** (3380 County Rd. 28, 607/535-9614, www.castelgrisch.com, hours vary seasonally, $16), a winery with a Swiss-style restaurant. Outside is a deck with lake views.

Blue Pointe Grille (16 N. Franklin St., 607/535-6116, www.watkinsglenharborhotel.com, $26) at Watkins Glen Harbor Hotel, is a casual fine dining restaurant where the talents of Chef Chris Hascall are expressed through signature dishes such as Rack of Lamb, Eggplant Strato, and Wild Mushroom Ravioli. The restaurant participates in Finger Lakes Culinary Bounty, a program where properties sign on to use freshly delivered locally grown products in their menus.

Nickel's Pit BBQ (205-207 N. Franklin St., 607/210-4227, www.nickelspitbbq.com, Wed.-Fri. 5pm-close, Sat.-Sun. noon-close, $11), located in the old Watkins Glen Fire Department building, serves authentic BBQ and craft beers. Its outdoor beer garden makes it an especially popular spot on weekends.

Village Marina Bar & Grill (Seneca Harbor Park, 607/535-7910, www.village-marina.com, hours vary seasonally, $9) is a hometown favorite located on the shore of Seneca Lake. Burgers and other bar food can be paired with local beer and wine. Summer weekends see plenty of live entertainment here.

Elmira

Elmira sits on both sides of the Chemung River, a few miles north of the Pennsylvania border. Some parts of the city are quite historic, with handsome stone and red-brick buildings.

Once the site of a Seneca village, Elmira was settled by Europeans in the 1780s. By the 1840s, the town was known for its lumbering and woolen mills, and by the 1860s, for its metal industries and iron furnaces. Elmira also served as a major transportation center, sitting at the crossroads of the Erie Railroad, the Chemung River, and the Chemung and Junction Canals.

Elmira has played an important role in the country's military and literary history. During the Civil War, the Union Army set up barracks in Elmira. In 1864, one of those barracks was turned into a prison camp for Confederate soldiers. The prison was poorly built and desperately overcrowded; thousands of prisoners died within a year.

Samuel Clemens, a.k.a. Mark Twain, spent more than 20 summers in Elmira. His wife, Olivia Langdon, grew up in the area and Twain wrote many of his masterpieces—including *Tom Sawyer* and *The Adventures of Huckleberry Finn*—while at the Langdon family farm.

Most of Elmira is north of the Chemung River. Exiting off Route 17 onto Route 352W (Church St.) will take you into the heart of the city. Route 14N runs past Elmira College and Woodlawn Cemetery (off West Woodlawn Ave.).

In July and August, hour-long **trolley tours**

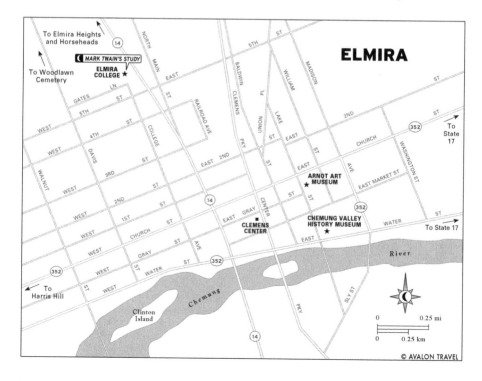

(Chemung County Chamber of Commerce, 607/734-5137 or 800/627-5892) of Elmira's historical attractions are offered.

SIGHTS
◖ Mark Twain's Study

The story of Mark Twain and Olivia Langdon began in 1867 when Twain fell in love with her after viewing her portrait, shown to him by a friend as they were crossing the Atlantic. Upon his return to the United States, Twain immediately set up a meeting with Olivia. At first, she was not at all impressed. He was a rough-and-tumble self-made man; she was a refined young woman from a good family.

But Twain was stubborn. For the next two years, he visited Elmira regularly, and eventually won over the entire Langdon family. In fact, near the end of his courtship, Olivia, who was sickly and delicate, was only allowed to visit with him for five minutes a day because she became so excited.

Mark Twain's Study (1 Park Pl., 607/735-1941, May 1-Labor Day Mon.-Sat. 9am-5pm and Sun. noon-5pm, Labor Day-Oct.15 Sat. 9am-5pm and Sun. noon-5pm, free), modeled after a Mississippi steamboat pilot house, was built for Twain by his sister-in-law. Twain once described it as "the loveliest study you ever saw. It is octagonal in shape with a peaked roof, each space filled with a spacious window and it sits perched in complete isolation on the very top of an elevation that commands leagues of valleys and city and retreating ranges of blue hill." In 1952, Twain's study was moved to its current location on the campus of Elmira College, one of the earliest colleges for women. The study's interior is simple and functional. A Remington Rand sits on a desk (Twain was one of the first writers to submit a typed manuscript to a publisher) and a trunk inscribed with the name "Clemens" rests on the floor. The author's hat and pipe rest on a desk. A student guide is stationed at the study and offers details and stories about its history.

Twain fans will want to visit several other campus spots, including statues dedicated to Twain and his wife. The Center for Mark Twain Studies hosts visiting scholars and annual symposia about the author's life, work, and influence.

Woodlawn Cemetery and Mark Twain Burial Site

In **Woodlawn Cemetery** (1200 Walnut St., 607/732-0151, daily dawn-dusk), Mark Twain is buried in the Langdon family plot, along with his wife, his father-in-law, and his son-in-law, Ossip Gabrilowitsch, a noted Russian-born pianist. A 12-foot-high monument commemorates the two famous men. Many visitors to Twain's grave consider their trip a pilgrimage and leave items like coins and cigars (Twain was known to smoke up to 22 cigars a day) on his tombstone.

Adjacent to the main cemetery is the **Woodlawn National Cemetery** (1825 Davis St., 607/732-5411, daily dawn-dusk), containing the graves of the 2,963 Confederate soldiers who died in the Elmira prison. Surrounding the Confederate graves are the graves of 322 Union soldiers. When families came north to retrieve their loved ones, they saw what respect had been afforded the soldiers and many made the decision to leave them in their resting place.

Arnot Art Museum

Arnot Art Museum (235 Lake St., at W. Gray St., 607/734-3697, www.arnotartmuseum.org, Tues.-Fri. 10am-5pm, Sat. noon-5pm, adults $7, seniors and students $5, children under 18 free), in a restored 1833 neoclassical mansion, displays a fine collection of 17th- to 19th-century European and 19th- to 20th-century American paintings. At the heart of the collection are works acquired by Matthias Arnot in the late 1800s. Among them are paintings by Brueghel, Daubigny, Rousseau, and Millet, hung floor to ceiling in the old salon style.

Behind the mansion, a handsome modern wing houses both temporary exhibitions and rotating selections from the museum's Asian, Egyptian, and pre-Columbian collections.

Chemung Valley History Museum

To learn more about Elmira'a past, visit the

© FRANCISCO COLLAZO

Mark Twain's grave at Woodlawn Cemetery in Elmira

Chemung Valley History Museum (415 E. Water St., 607/734-4167, www.chemungvalleymuseum.org, Mon.-Sat. 10am-5pm, adults $3, seniors $2, students 6-18 $1, children under 6 free). Exhibits on the Seneca, Mark Twain in Elmira, and the Civil War prison camp are featured. Trolley into Twain Country tours depart from the lobby throughout July and August. The tour is narrated by a guide.

◖ Harris Hill

Unassuming Elmira has been known as the Soaring Capital of America ever since 1930, when the first National Soaring Contest took place here. Today at **Harris Hill** (57 Soaring Hill Dr., 607/742-4213 or 607/734-0641, www.harrishillsoaring.org), you'll find **The National Soaring Museum, Harris Hill Soaring Center,** and **Harris Hill Amusement Park.** At the Soaring Museum, visitors can learn more about the history and sport of gliding, while the Soaring Center provides the opportunity to experience gliding, either through demonstrations or a gliding excursion. Visitors

who prefer to keep their feet on the ground can enjoy the rides and activities at the 27-acre amusement park, which features kiddie rides, batting cages, and go-karts. There is no admission fee; visitors pay by activity as they go along.

Wings of Eagles Discovery Center

Wings of Eagles Discovery Center (339 Daniel Zenker Dr., Horseheads, 607/358-4247, www.wingsofeagles.com, Tues.-Sat. 10am-4pm, adults $7, seniors $5.50, children 7-18 $4.50, children 6 and under free) is a 25,000-square-foot hangar where you can walk among or climb aboard a wide range of military aircraft dating from World War II to the present. On-site Wings Cafe ($9) serves soups, salads, flatbread pizzas, and sandwiches, the latter named after famous aircraft and aviators.

ACCOMMODATIONS AND CAMPING

A few miles south of Elmira lies **Newtown Battlefield State Park** (2346 Rte. 60,

607/732-6067, www.nysparks.com/parks/107, tent camping $15-21/night), where General John Sullivan won a decisive battle over a large force of Iroquois and Tories on August 19, 1779. Situated on a hilltop with wide-angled views of the Chemung Valley, the former battlefield is now a county park with hiking trails, a picnic area, and campgrounds.

Located between Elmira and Corning is **Rufus Tanner House Bed and Breakfast** (60 Sagetown Rd., Pine City, 607/732-0213, www. rufustanner.com, $130-150), a meticulously restored 1864 Greek Revival country home offering three spacious rooms with fireplaces and private baths. The B&B also has an outdoor garden and hot tub.

Elmira's Painted Lady Bed and Breakfast (520 W. Water St., 607/846-3500, www.elmiraspaintedlady.com, $170-230) is located near the Westside Historic District. Guests can't help but leave this lovely and lovingly-kept 1875 historic Victorian feeling like family due to the warmth of the excellent innkeepers who manage that perfect level of constant at-the-ready service without being obtrusive. A truly stellar and generous hot breakfast, tailored to guests' tastes, in-room fresh flowers, whirlpool soaking tubs, romantic fireplaces, the wide sitting porch, and 1880s billiard parlor where Mark Twain himself once puttered about make this a can't miss spot.

FOOD

Charlie's Café and Bakery (205 Hoffman St., 607/733-0440, www.charliescafeelmira.com) offers sandwiches, salads, soups, pastas, and Finger Lakes wine and beer in a casual but elegant dining room. Leave room for the Finger Lakes Harvest Wine Cake, a specialty of the restaurant and region. It features local ingredients, including Finger Lakes apples and, of course, Riesling.

Soup's On Café (311 College Ave., 607/398-7278, www.soupsoncafe-elmira.com, Mon.-Thurs. 10:30am-3:30pm, Fri. 10:30am-8pm, Sat. 7:30am-3:30pm, $7-10) is a great lunch stop, offering nearly a dozen homemade soups, along with wraps, sandwiches, burgers, and desserts. Wine and beer are also available.

Third-generation **Hill Top Inn Restaurant** (171 Jerusalem Hill Rd., 607/732-6728, $20) is just that and a friendly place to sit out on the large terrace and enjoy a gorgeous view of the valley below. It's just a stone's throw from the lookout where Mark Twain sat so inspired in the original location of his study. The spot is popular with locals and large loads of tourists stopping in as a midway point between Niagara and New York City. Fortunately, the establishment has the space to accommodate them all. Generous portions of items like Haystack Crab and a good-sized wine list keep the crowd happy.

Corning

If good things come in small packages, Corning is indeed a special present waiting for visitors to unwrap. One of the most popular tourist destinations in New York State, Corning is home to two exceptional museums, Rockwell Museum of Western Art and the more widely known Corning Museum of Glass, which, contrary to popular belief, does not exhibit Pyrex measuring cups or Corningware baking pans.

Corning, current population 11,108, became a one-industry town not long after 1868, when the Flint Glass Company of Brooklyn relocated here. The company chose Corning largely because of its strategic position on the Chemung River and Chemung Canal, which allowed for easy delivery of raw materials.

In 1875, the company began to produce specialized types of glass, such as railway signal lenses and thermometer tubing. In 1880, the light bulb division was developed in response to Edison's invention, and by the early 1930s, Corning was manufacturing 1,250,000 bulbs a day. In 1915, the company's research and development department invented Pyrex.

In the early 1970s, a fiber optics division was established.

Corning, Inc. remains a major employer in the area, but tourism is an increasingly important industry here, too.

SIGHTS
◖ Corning Museum of Glass

Billed as the world's largest museum devoted to glass, **Corning Museum of Glass** (1 Museum Way, 607/937-5371, www.cmog.org, Sept. 3-May 23 daily 9am-5pm, May 24-Sept. 2 daily 9am-8pm, adults $15, seniors and students $12.75, children under 19 free) features thousands of objects—including more than 1,000 paperweights and, of course, plenty of examples of Tiffany lampshades and windows—spanning 35 centuries. The museum's Glass Sculpture Gallery claims to be the largest display of glass in the world, showcasing more than 10,000 glass objects at a time, many dramatically displayed in darkened rooms with spotlights. The oldest objects date back to 1400 BC, the newest seen in famous designers' contributions to constantly changing installations. Among the many highlights are an iridescent vase from 10th-century Iran, an 11-foot-high Tiffany window, and a table-long glass boat cut by Baccarat in 1900. With over 40 daily shows (included in admission),

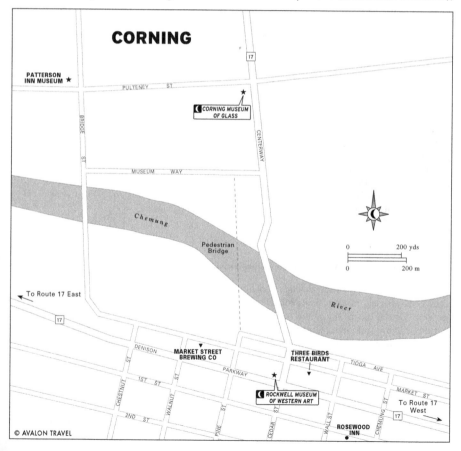

© AVALON TRAVEL

PHOTO COURTESY OF SCCVB

glass flowers at the Corning Museum of Glass

such as the Hot Glass Show, Flameworking Demos, and a demonstration where visitors can whip up a drawing and see it created out of glass in front of their eyes by a master gaffer, visitors can observe the art of glass up close. A **combination ticket** (adults $20, seniors and students $18.25) offers admission to both the Corning Museum of Glass and the Rockwell Museum.

The massive nonprofit gift shop, **GlassMarket,** is populated by the works of individual outside artisans, as well as pieces made by museum gaffers. Museum guests can also make their own souvenirs at **The Studio,** where visitors as young as three can participate in a brief glassmaking workshop. Classes start at $12 and include an impressively sturdy and beautiful object to bring home, each tailored to visitors' preferred style and colors. Create gorgeous ornaments like colorful blooms on deceptively delicate-looking stems by pulling molten glass into flower petals. Purchase tickets for designated time slots on entry to the museum or online.

Historic Market Street

After visiting the glass museum, most visitors stroll down a wide walkway that leads to Corning's historic downtown. This 19th-century district, called Corning Gaffer District, was extensively restored following Hurricane Agnes in 1972, when the street was all but destroyed by the flooding of Chemung River.

Today, Market Street is brick sidewalks, locust trees, and one bustling shop or restaurant after another. At one end are contemporary glass studios with artisans at work, including **Vitrix Hot Glass Studio** (77 W. Market St., 607/936-8707, Mon.-Fri. 9am-8pm, Sat. 10am-8pm, Sun. noon-5pm).

◖ Rockwell Museum of Western Art

Rockwell Museum of Western Art (111 Cedar St., 607/937-5386, www.rockwellmuseum.org, late May-early Sept. daily 9am-8pm, rest of the year daily 9am-5pm, adults $8, seniors and students $7, children under 19 free) has nothing to do with Norman Rockwell and everything

PHOTO COURTESY OF SCCVB

Corning's iconic tower

to do with art of the American West. Collected by Corning denizen Robert F. Rockwell, this is said to be the most comprehensive assemblage of Western art in the eastern United States. A **combination ticket** (adults $20, seniors and students $18.25) offers admission to both the Rockwell Museum and the Corning Museum of Glass.

The museum occupies the restored Old City Hall; permanent and temporary exhibits are well-curated in equally well-cared for galleries. Works by Frederic Remington, Charles M. Russell, and Albert Bierstadt hang from the walls, and Navajo rugs drape the stairwell. Exhibit cases contain Native American art and artifacts.

Rockwell was a passionate collector who once used the walls of his father's department store to exhibit his artwork, and the museum has an engaging, personal feel. The staff provides children with backpacks filled with fun, educational activities developed for each exhibit. This exceptionally family-friendly museum opened a kids' drawing room in 2013. The museum's gift shop is small, but has a thoughtful selection of art, jewelry, and handcrafts, most of which were made by Western artists, many of whom are Native American.

Benjamin Patterson Inn Museum Complex

A half mile north of Market Street is **Benjamin Patterson Inn Museum Complex** (59 W. Pulteney St., 607/937-5281, Mon.-Fri. 10am-4pm, adults $4, seniors $3, children and students $2), peopled by guides in costume dress. Restored historic buildings include Benjamin Patterson Inn Museum, complete with a women's parlor, tap room, and ballroom and the Painted Post-Erwin Museum, housed in a former freight depot.

ACCOMMODATIONS

One of the area's most popular B&Bs, the handsome **Rosewood Inn** (134 E. 1st St., 607/962-3253, www.rosewoodinn.com, $110-185), is located close to downtown. The five guest rooms and two suites are outfitted with antiques and have private baths. Downstairs is an elegant parlor with a fireplace, where afternoon tea is served.

Hillcrest Manor (227 Cedar St., 607/936-4548, www.corninghillcrestmanor.com, $155-185), located in an 1890s Greek Revival mansion, is a showplace for the area's art, which first drew the owners to visit Corning.

FOOD

Visit **Old World Cafe and Ice Cream** (1 W. Market St., 607/936-1953, www.oldworldcafe.com, spring and fall Mon.-Sat 10am-6pm, winter Mon.-Sat. 10am-5pm, summer Mon.-Sat. 10am-9pm and Sun. noon-5pm, $8) for hearty homemade soups, sandwiches, salad, old-fashioned candy, and ice cream. If grabbing a slice is more your taste, try **Atlas Brick Oven Pizzeria** (35 E. Market St., 607/962-2626, www.atlaspizzeria.com, Mon.-Thurs. 11am-10pm, Fri.-Sat. 11am-11pm, Sun. noon-10pm, $8). In addition to pizza, Atlas sells calzones, pasta, salads, and sandwiches.

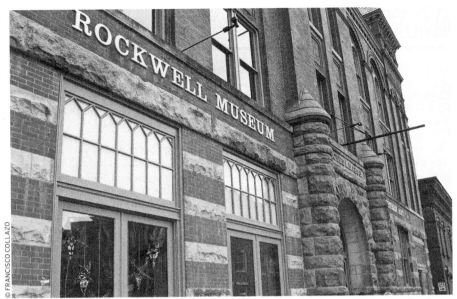

© FRANCISCO COLLAZO

the Rockwell Museum of Western Art

Locals love rustic, family-run **Spencer's** (359 E. Market St., 607/936-9196, daily 7am-10pm), popular for its homemade sticky buns and breakfast menu with only one or two options over the $5 mark.

Tiny, hidden **Bento Ya Masako** (31 E. Market St., 607/936-3659, Tues.-Fri. 11am-3pm, $9) is tucked between two jewelry shops, up a flight of stairs, and marked only by a small "Open" sign half-covering a Japanese symbol on a nondescript door. First timers might be caught off guard by the open kitchen at the top of the stairs in what looks like an apartment with two women cooking away. Just grab a seat at one of a handful of tables and prepare to be surprised. This cash-only establishment has limited hours, but offers authentic Japanese and sushi to those in the know.

Market Street Brewing Co. (63 W. Market St., 607/936-2337, www.936-beer.com, Mon.-Sat. 11:30am-10pm, Sun. noon-9pm, $18) offers something for everyone, including rooftop and biergarten dining, dishes ranging from salads to steaks, a kids' menu, and, of course, fresh brews on tap. The casually elegant **Three Birds Restaurant and Martini Bar** (73 E. Market St., 607/936-8862, www.threebirdsrestaurant.com, restaurant Mon.-Sat. 5pm-10pm, martini bar Mon.-Sat. 4pm-1am, $22) serves "progressive American fare" made with fresh local ingredients. It's also known for its popular martini bar.

The Cellar (21 W. Market St., 607/377-5552, www.corningwinebar.com, Mon.-Thurs. 5pm-9pm, Fri.-Sat. 5pm-10pm, Sun. 10:30am-3pm, $30) is an elegant wine bar and modern fusion restaurant, offering plates focused on locally-sourced ingredients.

Keuka Lake

Gentle, Y-shaped Keuka Lake is the only one of the Finger Lakes with an irregular outline, made up of over 70 miles of curving lakeshore, scalloped with coves and bays. Its name means "canoe landing" in Iroquois.

At the southern head of Keuka Lake lies Hammondsport, site of one of the nation's first wineries, established in 1860. The small town Penn Yan occupies the lake's northern tip. Several Mennonite communities are scattered throughout the Keuka Lake region. Driving south between Penn Yan and Dundee along Routes 14A or 11, or north of Penn Yan along Routes 14A, 374, and 27, you're bound to pass a horse-and-buggy or two clip-clopping down the road. Handwritten signs advertising Mennonite quilts, furniture, or produce for sale sometimes appear by the roadside, while more permanent shops are located near Penn Yan and Dundee.

HAMMONDSPORT

Nestled between steep, verdant hills and Keuka Lake, Hammondsport is a fetching Victorian village with a lively tourist trade. At its center lies the village square, anchored by a charming white Presbyterian church. Antique shops, cafés, and restaurants line Shethar Street, the main drag. A park and two public beaches are along the lakeshore; the beach at the foot of Shethar Street is said to be the best. It is the local viticulture, though, that draws the most visitors. Tumbling down the surrounding hillsides are vineyard after vineyard, all supplying grapes for the area's 17 wineries.

Glenn Hammond Curtiss, the pioneer aviator, was born in Hammondsport in 1878. Though not as well known as the Wright brothers, Curtiss made the world's first pre-announced flight on July 4, 1908 when he piloted his "June Bug" airplane over 5,090 feet just outside Hammondsport. Curtiss developed the U.S. Navy's first amphibian airplane, opened the first flying school in America, and

established the Curtiss Aeroplane Company—all in Hammondsport. During World War I, the Curtiss company manufactured the popular Curtiss Jenny airplane, which later became a favorite of barnstormers.

Great Western Winery Visitor Center

Even if you're the odd Finger Lakes visitor who isn't interested in wine, you might want to stop by the **Great Western Winery Visitor Center** (8260 Pleasant Valley Rd./County Rd. 88, 607/569-6111, www.pleasantvalleywine.com, Apr.-Dec. daily 10am-5pm, Jan.-Mar. Tues.-Sat. 10am-4pm, free, tours $5 per person), one of the largest tourist attractions in the region. The Pleasant Valley Wine Company, better known as the Great Western Winery, is one of the oldest continuous makers of wine in the United States, founded by a group of Hammondsport businessmen in 1860.

The visitor center holds exhibits that explain

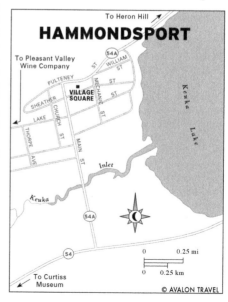

AMONG THE MENNONITES

A surprisingly large number of Mennonite and Amish Mennonite communities are scattered throughout the Finger Lakes and Western New York. Some were established generations ago, but many others were set up more recently by people from Pennsylvania and Ohio who were attracted to New York by its numerous abandoned family farms.

The Mennonite religion is a Protestant sect, founded by Dutch reformer Menno Simons in Switzerland in the 1500s. The Amish are the Mennonites' most conservative branch, established in Pennsylvania in the 18th century. Both groups shun modern society and technology.

An especially large Amish population lives in Cattaraugus County in Western New York, but a growing number of Mennonites are settling in Yates, Schuyler, and Ontario Counties in the Finger Lakes. Local residents estimate that the Mennonite population in these three counties—all centered around Keuka Lake—has increased exponentially since the late 1970s; in Yates County alone, there are more than 520 Mennonite families.

Throughout the region, you'll see Amish driving their horse and buggies, and you'll spot occasional signs advertising handmade quilts, furniture, or baskets for sale. Though not as organized as Western New York, whose Amish participate in the Amish Trail program for visitors, the Finger Lakes' Amish and Mennonite communities are still accessible to visitors. Travelers can purchase goods at Amish farms throughout the region. Good places to stop include The Windmill Farm and Craft Market and Oak Hill Bulk Foods and Cafe, both near Penn Yan.

The Amish and Mennonites dislike having their pictures taken. Please respect their wishes. Also, be aware that they do not work on Sundays, so their farms and shops will be closed on that day.

the history of the winery and the region, as well as an informative film, which is screened inside a 35,000-gallon former wine tank. A nearby working model train replicates the old Bath-Hammondsport Railroad, and a tasting room offers products for sampling. Winery tours are offered throughout the day. Take the hour-long tour through magnificent stone winery buildings, eight of which are listed on the National Register of Historic Places. The tour ends with a wine tasting.

Wine Tasting

One of the odder tales in the chronicles of Finger Lakes viticulture is that of the battle waged over the name Taylor. Walter S. Taylor, a grandson of the founder of the Taylor Wine Co., was kicked out of the company in 1970. Subsequently, he and his father Greyton began their own winery high on Bully Hill. In 1977, Coca-Cola bought the Taylor Wine Co. and sued Walter for using his family name on his own labels. The case went to court and Walter lost, only to become a local hero. "They have my name and heritage but they didn't get my goat!" he proclaimed and flamboyantly struck out the Taylor name on all his labels. "Branded For Life, by a man that shall remain nameless without Heritage" reads the byline in his brochures. The **Wine and Grape Museum of Greyton H. Taylor** (8843 G.H. Taylor Memorial Dr., 607/868-3610, www.bullyhillvineyards.com, Wed.-Sun. 11am-5pm, free) tells little of this story. Instead, it focuses on antique winemaking equipment and the delicate, lyrical Bully Hill labels, all drawn by "Walter St. Bully." Adjacent to the museum are **Bully Hill Vineyards,** open for tastings. Also on site is Bully Hill Restaurant, offering great views of the lake.

Dr. Frank's Vinifera Wine Cellars (9749 Middle Rd., 607/868-4884, www.DrFrankWines.com, Mon.-Sat. 9am-5pm, Sun. noon-5pm, tastings free) was one of the first in the region to grow the European Vinifera grape. Dr. Frank was an immigrant from Ukraine who arrived in the Finger Lakes in 1962. Today, his family still runs the winery, best known for their multiple award-winning chardonnays and Rieslings.

A few miles beyond Dr. Frank's is **Heron Hill Winery** (9301 Rte. 76, 607/868-4241, www.heronhill.com, Mon.-Sat. 10am-5pm, Sun. noon-5pm). Opened in 1977, it specializes in chardonnays, Rieslings, and Concord grape juice for the kids. Heron Hill also operates a café in the summer. Enjoy views of the lake and the vineyards from its deck.

Glenn H. Curtiss Museum

The cavernous hangars of the former Curtiss Aeroplane Company now contain the sprawling **Glenn H. Curtiss Museum** (8419 Rte. 54, 607/569-2160, www.glennhcurtissmuseum.org, May 1-Oct. 31 Mon.-Sat. 9am-5pm and Sun. 10am-5pm, Nov. 1-Apr. 30 daily 10am-4pm, adults $8.50, seniors $7, children 7-18 $5.50), devoted to both Curtiss and the early history of aviation. About a dozen spiffy antique airplanes crowd the main hall, along with antique bicycles, motorcycles, propellers, and engines. Curtiss's first interest was the bicycle. One of his earliest planes, the Curtiss Pusher, looks just like a bike with double wings and wires attached.

A highlight of the museum is a replica of the famous "June Bug" airplane, built by volunteers in the mid-1970s. A Curtiss Jenny and delicate Curtiss Robin—resembling a giant grasshopper—stand nearby.

Accommodations

Vinehurst Inn and Suites (7988 Rte. 54, 607/569-2300, www.vinehurstinn.com, $110-160) features spacious motel rooms, many with cathedral ceilings. Suites, including three for families and three with whirlpool tubs, are also available.

Lake & Vine Bed and Breakfast (61 Lake St., 607/569-3282, www.lakeandvinebb.info, $125-150), an 1868 Queen Anne style home, offers four rooms, candlelit gourmet breakfast served with china and crystal, and many modern amenities.

Black Sheep Inn (8329 Pleasant Valley Rd., 607/569-3767, www.stayblacksheepinn.com, $155-275) is a five-room boutique inn, offering indulgent organic breakfasts utilizing local and organic products. This historic octagonal house also features an on-site spa.

About 15 miles away, in the village of Avoca, is a bit of novelty: the storybook **C Caboose Motel** (8620 Rte. 415, 607/566-2216, www.caboosemotel.net, $75). Here, you can sleep in snug, restored 1916 train cabooses outfitted with modern conveniences.

Food

In addition to its mouth-watering ice-cream treats, cozy **Crooked Lake Ice Cream Parlor** (33 Shethar St., 607/569-2405) serves a good breakfast and lunch.

As its name suggests, **The Waterfront Restaurant** (12664 W. Lake Rd., 607/868-3455, www.waterfrontkeuka.com, Mon.-Fri. 4pm-close, Sat.-Sun. noon-close, $16) offers lakeside dining. Specials are featured every night of the week. The Original Clammin' and Jammin' happens on the dock every Sunday, Memorial Day through Labor Day, with fresh steamed clams and free live music.

PENN YAN

Named for its early Pennsylvanian and Yankee settlers, Penn Yan is an attractive small town (pop. 5,131) that serves as the seat of Yates County. Its claim to fame is the world's largest pancake.

Birkett Mills

On a windowless wall of **Birkett Mills** (1 Main St., www.thebirkettmills.com), an enormous griddle is mounted alongside the words: "The annual Buckwheat Harvest Festival. Size of big griddle used to make world record pancake, Sept. 27, 1987. 28 feet, 1 inch." What more needs to be said? Established in 1797 and in continuous operation ever since, Birkett Mills is the world's largest producer of buckwheat products and maintains a small **retail shop** (163 Main St., 315/536-3311) in its offices.

© FRANCISCO COLLAZO

vineyards at Heron Hill Winery

Oliver House Museum

Oliver House Museum (200 Main St., 315/536-7318, www.yatespast.com, Tues.-Fri. 9am-4pm, free), housed in a handsome brick building, is run by the Yates County History Center. Permanent and temporary exhibits are on display, interpreting a variety of regional historical and cultural themes.

Recreation

The proprietors of *The Esperanza Rose* (481 Mill St., Branchport, 315/595-6618, www.esperanzaboat.com), a 65-foot, 85-ton wooden cruising yacht, offer lake excursions. In addition to sightseeing trips, lunch and dinner cruises are offered. The boat departs from its dock on Mill Street in the town of Branchport, about a 10-minute drive from Penn Yan.

Events

Yates County Fair takes over Penn Yan fairgrounds in mid-July. On the Fourth of July and the Saturday before Labor Day, the shores of Keuka Lake glow with magical **Rings of Fire,** as in the days of the Seneca. The Seneca lit bonfires to celebrate the harvest; today, highway flares celebrate the holidays. For information about any of these events, contact the **Yates County Chamber of Commerce** (315/536-3111, www.yatesny.com).

Shopping

Midway between Penn Yan and Dundee is **Windmill Farm and Craft Market** (3900 Rte. 14A, 315/536-3032, www.thewindmill.com, late Apr.-mid-Dec. Sat. 8am-4:30pm), the oldest and biggest of several indoor/outdoor farm-and-crafts markets operating in the Finger Lakes. Every Saturday, from the last Saturday in April to the second Saturday in December, more than 200 local vendors set up shop in a large fairgrounds area off Route 14A. Produce, flowers, furniture, crafts, wine, antiques, and homemade food are among the goods for sale. Many Mennonite families operate booths here.

In Dundee, you'll find **Martin's Kitchen** (4898 John Green Rd., 607/243-8197), selling homemade pickles, pickled watermelon rinds, jams, apple butter, and other Mennonite specialties.

Accommodations and Food

Cozy **Fox Inn** (158 Main St., 315/536-3101, www.foxinnbandb.com, $155-180), near downtown, is an 1820s Greek Revival home with five guest rooms and a carriage house loft. Common areas include a parlor with billiards table, a sitting room with a wood-burning fireplace, and a rose garden.

Merritt Hill Manor (2756 Coates Rd., 315/536-7682, www.merritthillmanor.com, $165-189) is situated on an 18-acre estate with great views of both Keuka and Seneca Lakes. The 1822 country manor offers five guest rooms, a breezy porch, and a living room with a fireplace.

Diner aficionados will want to stop by the classic **Penn Yan Diner** (131 E. Elm St., 315/536-6004, www.pennyandiner.com, Tues.-Sat. 7am-7pm, Sun. 7am-1pm, $12), which dates back to 1925.

Canandaigua Lake

The farthest west of the major Finger Lakes, Canandaigua is also the most commercialized. Rochester is less than 30 miles away, and the lake has served as that city's summer playground since the late 1800s. At the northern end of the lake is the historic city of Canandaigua, now largely a resort town. At the southern end is the village of Naples.

Canandaigua is Iroquois for "The Chosen Place." According to legend, the Seneca people were born at the south end of the lake, on South Hill. The Creator caused the ground to open, allowing the Seneca to climb out. All went well until a giant serpent coiled itself around the base of the hill. Driven by an insatiable hunger, the snake picked off the Seneca one by one until at last a young warrior slew him with a magic arrow. The dying serpent writhed down the hill, disgorging the heads of its victims as he went; large rounded stones resembling human skulls have been found in the area. South Hill is now part of the Hi Tor Wildlife Management Area.

Also connected with the Seneca is tiny Squaw Island, located in the northern end of the lake. Many women and children escaped slaughter by hiding here during General Sullivan's 1779 campaign.

CANANDAIGUA

The city of Canandaigua has a wide, expansive feel. Busy Main Street, a four-lane thoroughfare lined with leafy trees and imposing Greek Revival buildings, runs through its center. The lake and City Pier are at the foot of Main. Tourist-oriented businesses dominate.

Following the Revolution, two New Englanders, Oliver Phelps and Nathaniel Gorham, purchased what is now Canandaigua, along with the rest of western New York, from the Native Americans. Settlers arrived in 1789, and shortly thereafter, the first land office in the United States was established near present-day Main Street.

On November 11, 1794, Seneca chiefs and General Timothy Pickering met in Canandaigua to sign what was later known as the Pickering Treaty. A document of enormous significance, the treaty granted whites the right to settle the Great Lakes Basin. An original copy of the treaty can be found in the Ontario County Historical Society Museum.

Sonnenberg Gardens and Mansion

A serene 50-acre garden estate, **Sonnenberg Gardens and Mansion** (151 Charlotte St., 585/394-4922, www.sonnenberg.org, May 1-May 26 and Sept. 3-Oct. 31 daily 9:30am-4:30pm, May 27-Sept. 2 daily 9:30am-5:30pm, adults $12, seniors $10, students 13-17 $6, children 4-12 $1, children under 4 free), sits in the heart of the bustling downtown. The Smithsonian Institution credited the place "one

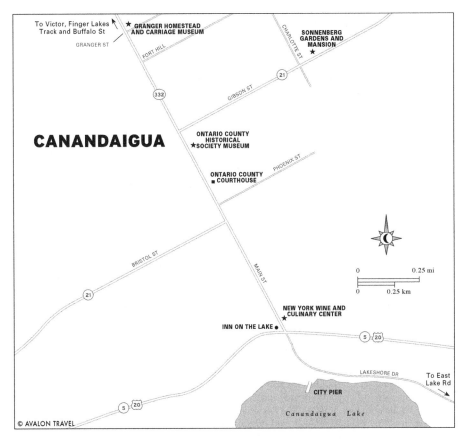

of the most magnificent late-Victorian gardens ever created in America," thanks to its nine formal gardens, an arboretum, a turn-of-the-20th-century greenhouse, and a massive 1887 stone mansion.

Sonnenberg (German for "Sunny Hill") was once the summer home of Mary Clark and Frederick Ferris Thompson. Thompson, whose father helped establish Chase Bank, was co-founder of the First National City Bank of New York City.

The estate's nine gardens were created by Mrs. Thompson as a memorial after her husband's death in 1899. A classic rose garden features over 4,000 rose bushes, and the Japanese Garden took seven workers six months to create. The secluded Sub Rosa Garden contains statues of Zeus, Diana, and Apollo. The Blue & White Garden contains only blue and white flowers.

Visitors to Sonnenberg can wander freely—even the mansion is self-guided—though guided walking tours are also offered June-September. Near the entrance is an inviting café, housed in one of the greenhouses, and the huge, commercial **Finger Lakes Wine Center** (585/394-9016, May-Oct. daily 11am-4pm), selling regional wines.

Granger Homestead and Carriage Museum

The 1816 Federal-style **Granger Homestead**

and Carriage Museum (295 N. Main St., 585/394-1472, www.grangerhomestead.org, Tues., Wed., and Sun. 1pm-5pm, Thurs.-Sat. 11am-5pm, adults $6, seniors $5, students $2) once housed Gideon Granger, U.S. postmaster general under Presidents Jefferson and Madison. The home, which Granger once boasted was "unrivalled in all the nation," is especially notable for its elaborate carved moldings and mantelpieces, and for its fine original furnishings.

Dark, towering trees surround the house. Out back is a carriage museum, packed with about 50 spit-and-polish coaches, sporting carriages, sleighs, commercial wagons, and an undertaker's hearse.

Ontario County Historical Museum

To learn more about the history of Canandaigua, step into the **Ontario County Historical Museum** (55 N. Main St., 585/394-4975, www.ochs.org, Tues.-Fri. 10am-4:30pm, Sat. 11am-3pm, free, donations accepted), situated in a handsome brick building. On display is the original Six Nations' copy of the Pickering Treaty with the signatures of Iroquois leaders Red Jacket, Cornplanter, Handsome Lake, Farmer's Brother, Little Beard, and Fish Carrier. Each signed with an X. The museum also features "life masks" of Abraham Lincoln (plaster-of-Paris masks taken from a mold of his face), a small children's discovery area, and temporary exhibits.

Ontario County Courthouse

Dominating downtown Canandaigua, and indeed much of the surrounding countryside, is the bulbous dome of **Ontario County Courthouse** (27 N. Main St., at Gorham, 585/396-4200, Mon.-Fri. 8:30am-5pm). A marvelous collection of portraits hangs in the two courtrooms of this 1858 Greek Revival structure. Among them are likenesses of Red Jacket and Susan B. Anthony, who was tried here in 1873 for voting in the national election in Rochester. She was found guilty and fined $100. A boulder on the courthouse grounds

commemorates the Pickering Treaty, signed here in 1794.

New York Wine and Culinary Center

A treat for foodies, **New York Wine and Culinary Center** (800 S. Main St., 585/394-7070, www.nywcc.com, Wed.-Thurs. and Sun. 11am-6pm, Fri.-Sat. 11am-8pm) is a beautiful 20,000-square-foot facility housing a tempting boutique with food products and kitchen tools for culinary-minded visitors. The center also has a glass-walled educational theater where classes and demos can be observed and the occasional food show is filmed. There is an impressive **Tasting Center** featuring the state's finest wines, beers, and spirits in a warm wood and stone setting. At **Upstairs Bistro,** locally farmed ingredients come together in excellent meals with suggested wine and beer pairings that bring out the fullest flavors of the food. Visitors sticking around for a day or two can also sign up for a cooking class.

Live music makes weekend evenings a great time to visit for beer lovers, as a rotating selection of brews, chosen from New York's burgeoning number of craft breweries, are featured on tap (flight tasting available), as well as bottle choices from the state. New York State Charcuterie Sampler and Artisan Cheese Plate are two good choices for nibbling.

Recreation

The *Canandaigua Lady* (205 Lakeshore Dr., 585/396-7350, www.steamboatlandingresort. com, May-Oct.) is a 150-passenger paddlewheel boat offering lunch, afternoon, and dinner cruises.

For a more active experience on the lake, **Canandaigua Sailboarding** (11 Lakeshore Dr., 585/394-8150, www.cdgasailboard.com, daily 10am-6pm) rents kayaks, stand-up paddleboards, and water-bikes. The staff also gives windsurfing lessons during the summer.

In winter, **Bristol Mountain Winter Resort** (5662 Rte. 64, 585/374-1100, www. bristolmountain.com), at 1,200-feet, claims to have the highest vertical rise between the

Adirondacks and the Rocky Mountains. Thirty-four slopes and trails represent a varied terrain, offering skiing and snowboarding opportunities for novices as well as experts. Several local hotels and bed-and-breakfast lodgings partner with the ski resort, offering free passes to Bristol Mountain with a one-night stay.

Seven miles northwest of Canandaigua is **Finger Lakes Gaming & Racetrack** (5857 Rte. 96, 585/924-3232, www.fingerlakesracetrack.com). Thoroughbred racing takes place April-November Friday-Tuesday. Also on-site are more than 1,200 gaming machines. The already ample casino expanded exponentially in late 2013 with the addition of 33,000 square feet of space, which included a new bar and restaurant, among other gaming installations.

Entertainment

During the summer, Rochester Philharmonic Orchestra performs regularly at **Constellation Brands–Marvin Sands Performing Arts Center (CMAC)** (3355 Marvin Sands Dr., 585/394-4400, www.cmacevents.com), an outdoor amphitheater with 10,000 lawn seats and 5,000 covered seats. Rock, jazz, and pop-music concerts are sometimes presented as well.

Accommodations

The Canandaigua region is home to many luxury B&Bs. One of the best is the snug, colonial-style ◖ **1795 Acorn Inn** (4508 Rte. 64, Bristol Center, 585/229-2834, www.acorninnbb.com, $170-275), which has achieved the AAA four-diamond rating for nearly 20 years, a rarity for a B&B. Once a stagecoach stop, the inn now pampers guests with comfy canopy beds, luxurious private baths, an outdoor hot tub, and multi-course breakfasts.

The Inn on the Lake (770 S. Main St., 585/394-7800, www.theinnonthelake.com, $152-255) is a full-service hotel and conference center. Among its features are 134 nicely appointed guest rooms, many with patios or balconies; a pristine outdoor pool; saunas; and the airy, inviting restaurant, The Shore. The restaurant looks out to the lake and tiny

Squaw Island. Just 20 by 50 yards, the wild, tree-covered spot where Native Americans were said to have placed their women and children for safety during skirmishes can be reached by kayak (Canandaigua Sailboarding, 585/394-8150, www.cdgasailboard.com).

Not too far away is plush 1810 **Morgan-Samuels B&B Inn** (2920 Smith Rd., 585/394-9232, www.morgansamuelsinn.com, $169-325), which also holds the coveted AAA four-diamond rating. Here, you'll have your choice of one among six guest rooms, all of which are decorated in a Victorian antique style. The inn has eight fireplaces, tennis courts, and serves gourmet breakfast by candlelight. A six-course dinner is available by request for an additional fee.

Bristol Harbour Resort (5410 Seneca Point Rd., 585/396-2200, www.bristol-harbour.com, $185-495) is a 31-room, Adirondack-style resort that sits on Bristol Mountain, a perch offering spectacular lake views. The resort also has cottages and condos for rent. Golfers particularly enjoy this resort, as it has an 18-hole championship golf course designed by Robert Trent Jones. Other amenities and services include a spa, a restaurant, a private marina and beach, and a year-round hot tub.

Food

Il Posto Bistro and Wine Bar (137 S. Main St., 585/905-0535, www.ilpostobistroandwinebar.com, Tues.-Thurs. 5pm-9pm, Fri.-Sat. 5pm-10pm, $17) is a small, intimate restaurant specializing in Italian cuisine. It has a robust wine list, though few of the wines are from the area; most are from Italy and France.

The Shore (770 S. Main St., 585/394-7800, $26), located at The Inn on the Lake, offers great views of the lake and contemporary American fare.

The Office Restaurant (2574 Macedon Rd., 585/394-8787, www.ericsofficerestaurant.com, Mon.-Sat. 11am-midnight, $16) is especially worth keeping in mind if you're looking for a late night meal, as it's open until midnight. Burgers, bar fare, and heavier American entrées (think tenderloin topped with bleu cheese) are on offer here.

VICTOR

About 10 miles northwest of Canandaigua sprawls the village of Victor, worth visiting because an important Seneca village once stood here. The village was home to about 4,500 people; its palisaded granary stored hundreds of thousands of bushels of corn. All was destroyed in 1687 by a French army, led by the governor of Canada, who wanted to eliminate the Seneca as competitors in the fur trade.

Ganondagan State Historic Site

A visit to **Ganondagan State Historic Site** (1488 Rte. 444, 585/742-1690, www.ganondagan.org, May 1-Sept. 30 Tues.-Sun. 9am-5pm, Oct. Tues.-Sat. 9am-5pm, adults $3, children $2), which means "Town of Peace," begins with an interesting video that tells the story of the Seneca Nation and that of Jikohnsaseh, or Mother of Nations. Together with "The Peacemaker" and Hiawatha, Jikohnsaseh was instrumental in forging the Five Nations Confederacy; it was she who proposed that the Onondangan chief, who at first refused to join the confederacy, be appointed chairman of the Chiefs' Council. Jikohnsaseh once lived in the vicinity of Ganondagan and is believed to be buried nearby. No one searches for her grave, however, as a sign of respect.

Three trails that lead over gentle terrain past informative plaques begin just outside the visitor center. The Trail of Peace relates important moments in Seneca history. The Earth of Our Mother Trail identifies plants important to the Seneca. The Granary Trail recreates the day in 1687 that Ganondagan was destroyed, through journal entries from the French forces. There is also a replica of a 17th-century bark longhouse on site.

Food

Warfield's (3 Coulter Ln., Clifton Springs, 315/462-7184, www.warfields.com, Tues.-Sat. 11:30am-2:30pm and 5pm-9pm, $24) features seasonal "country fare" inflected with Asian

and European influences, served in a dining room with a pressed tin ceiling.

Lucca Wood-Fire Bistro (90 W. Main St., Victor, 585/924-9009, www.luccawfpizza.com, Wed.-Thurs. 11:30am-8pm, Fri. 11:30am-9pm, Sat. noon-9pm, Sun. noon-7pm, $11) serves pizzas crisped to perfection in its wood-fired oven, as well as panini and salads.

PALMYRA

About 15 miles due north of Canandaigua is Palmyra, an old Erie Canal town where Joseph Smith allegedly received a set of gold tablets inscribed with the Book of Mormon from the angel Moroni. The Hill Cumorah Pageant commemorates that event every July.

Downtown Palmyra is small and compact, lined with sturdy brick buildings. A church stands at each corner of the intersection of Main Street and Route 21, a fact that once made it into *Ripley's Believe It or Not.* Just west of downtown is the graceful stone **Erie Canal Aqueduct,** off Route 31.

Three small museums run by Historic Palmyra sit side-by-side downtown. On the outskirts of town are the Hill Cumorah Visitor Center and Joseph Smith Farm, run by the Mormon Church.

Historic Palmyra

A **trail ticket** (adults $7, seniors and children $5) offers admission to all four historic Palmyra museums. **William Phelps General Store and Home Museum** (140 Market St., 315/597-6981, www.historicpalmyrany.com, May 1-Oct. 31 Tues.-Sat. 10:30am-4:30pm, Nov. 1-Apr. 30 Tues.-Thurs. 11am-4pm, adults $3, seniors and children 12-17 $2, children under 12 free) was operated by the Phelps family from the 1860s until the 1940s. The museum recreates the general store of the 1890s and is an incredible untouched place to poke around, with excellent guides leading the way back into a simpler time. Shelves feature, among other items, spices and extracts that have retained their scents.

The **Alling Coverlet Museum** (122 William St., 315/597-6981, www.historicpalmyrany.com, Mon.-Sat. 1pm-4pm, adults $3, seniors

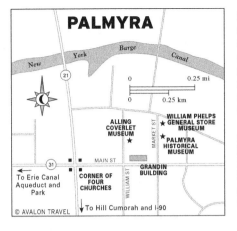

PALMYRA

New York Barge Canal

© AVALON TRAVEL

To Erie Canal Aqueduct and Park

ALLING COVERLET MUSEUM
WILLIAM PHELPS GENERAL STORE MUSEUM
PALMYRA HISTORICAL MUSEUM
MAIN ST
CORNER OF FOUR CHURCHES
GRANDIN BUILDING
To Hill Cumorah and I-90

and children 12-17 $2, children under 12 free) houses the largest collection of handwoven coverlets in the United States. Often referred to as the American tapestry, coverlets are ornate bed coverings made out of wool, cotton, or linen.

The nearby **Palmyra Historical Museum** (132 Market St., 315/597-6981, www.historic-palmyrany.com, May 1-Oct. 31 Tues.-Sat. 10:30am-4:30pm, Nov. 1-Apr. 30 Tues.-Thurs. 11am-4pm, adults $3, seniors and children 12-17 $2, children under 12 free) occupies the former St. James Hotel. Exhibits here include 19th-century furniture, Erie Canal art and artifacts, children's toys, stern Victorian portraits, and a tour led by an expressive guide who brings the historic objects to life with animated anecdotes.

Palmyra Print Shop (140 Market St., 315/597-6981, www.historicpalmyrany.com, May 1-Oct. 31 Tues.-Sat. 10:30am-4:30pm, Nov. 1-Apr. 30 Tues.-Thurs. 11am-4pm, adults $3, seniors and children 12-17 $2, children under 12 free) features Palmyra-made printing presses and cutters with handmade type and print blocks from 1838 through 1972.

Hill Cumorah Visitor Center

A good place to learn about the Mormon religion is at the **Hill Cumorah Visitor Center** (603 Rte. 21, 315/597-5851, www.hillcumorah.com, Mon.-Sat. 9am-9pm, Sun. noon-9pm, free),

four miles south of downtown. Most visitors are Mormons, but non-Mormons are welcome and are left more or less in peace to peruse the exhibits. A film provides a good introduction to Mormon history and beliefs, and exhibits tout the growth of the religion. There are currently about nine million Mormons worldwide, though only 1,500 live in upstate New York.

Behind the center stands Hill Cumorah, the drumlin where Joseph Smith is said to have found the gold tablets on September 22, 1827. It took him years to translate the tablets, and after he was done, he reburied them. A gold statue of the angel Moroni sits atop Hill Cumorah.

Joseph Smith Farm and Sacred Grove

Born in Vermont in 1805, Joseph Smith first came to Palmyra with his family in 1815. The Smiths were farmers, and Joseph—described by one contemporary as a "quiet, low-speaking, unlaughing" boy—lived in this simple, white clapboard house, now known as the **Joseph Smith Farm** (29 Stafford Rd., 315/597-5851, www.hillcumorah.com, Mon.-Sat. 9am-7pm, Sun. 12:30pm-7pm, free), until he was 22. He received his first vision in the **Sacred Grove** behind the house when he was only 14.

Events

The largest outdoor pageant in the United States, the **Hill Cumorah Pageant** (www.hillcumorah.org/Pageant) commemorates Joseph Smith's visitation from the angel Moroni, which led to the founding of the Mormon religion. It's a spectacular performance with a cast and technological special effects worthy of Broadway.

Each August Palmyra hosts the **Wayne County Fair** (www.waynecountyfair.org), one of the oldest fairs in the country, having originated in 1849. Livestock displays and beauty pageants are just two of the many activities at this beloved fair.

Palmyra Canaltown Days (www.palmyra-canaltowndays.org) celebrates the town's historic connection to the Erie Canal. Held every

September, the festival features craft and food vendors, and draws thousands of visitors.

Accommodations

A generous breakfast and kind hosts make **Liberty House** (131 W. Main St., Palmyra, 315/597-0011, www.libertyhousebb.com, $89-99) particularly noteworthy; the affordable rates don't hurt, either. Three guest rooms are available in this beautiful Victorian home with a wrap-around porch.

Palmyra Inn (955 Canandaigua Rd., 800/426-9900, www.palmyrainn.com, $119-199) offers 60 rooms and suites, with kitchenettes in each room. Amenities include free wireless Internet access, a whirlpool tub and exercise room, and deluxe continental breakfast.

SOUTH ON ROUTES 364 AND 245

Heading south down Canandaigua's eastern shore, you'll pass through a series of picturesque valleys. At the southern end of the lake, the route skirts around South Hill and **High Tor Wildlife Management Area** (585/226-2466). Hiking trails traverse the preserve, which is also one of the few places left in New York where you can still spot Eastern bluebirds, the state bird. The main entrance to the area is off Route 245 between Middlesex and Naples.

NAPLES

Just south of Canandaigua Lake, surrounded by hills, lies Naples (pop. 2,500). A tidy village with a brisk tourist trade, Naples centers around a historic **Old Town Square.** Naples is one of the best places in the Finger Lakes to sample a sweet regional specialty: grape pie. The pies, made with dark grapes, are best during fall harvest season.

Wineries

The local grapes are used for something more than pie. **Hazlitt's Red Cat Cellars** (5712 Rte. 414, 607/546-9463, www.hazlitt1852.com) hosts wine-tastings in its wood-paneled tasting room. **Inspire Moore Winery and Vineyard** (197 N. Main St., 585/374-5970, www.

inspiremoorewinery.com) has a casual restaurant next to the winery. **Arbor Hill Grapery** (6461 Rte. 64, 583/374-2870, www.thegrapery.com) features a shop and **Brew & Brats,** a restaurant specializing in exactly what its name suggests.

Cumming Nature Center

About eight miles northwest of the village lies 900-acre **Cumming Nature Center** (6472 Gulick Rd., 585/374-6160, www.rmsc.org, Wed.-Fri. 9am-3:30pm, Sat.-Sun. 9am-4:30pm, $3), owned by the Rochester Museum and Science Center. A veritable outdoor museum, the preserve holds six miles of themed trails leading through forests and wetlands. The Conservation Trail illustrates theories of forest management; the Pioneer Trail, complete with a reconstructed homestead, teaches about the early settlers' lives. The Beaver Trail focuses on the principles of ecology, and the Iroquois Trail focuses on Native American life. A visitors' center is near the entrance.

Gannett Hill

Scenic Route 21 heads due north out of Naples to the highest point in Ontario County: Gannett Hill, 2,256 feet above sea level. Now part of Ontario County Park, the hill offers bird's-eye views of the surrounding countryside.

Entertainment

The only performing arts venue of its kind in the immediate area, **Bristol Valley Theater** (151 S. Main St., 585/374-6318, www.bvtnaples.org) is housed inside an old church. Music, theater, dance, comedy, and children's events are staged in spring, summer, and fall.

Shopping

At **Artizanns** (118 N. Main St., 585/374-6740, www.artizanns.com), more than 200 Finger Lakes artists and artisans exhibit their wares for purchase, with pottery, jewelry, photography, paintings, metalwork, and much more on display.

Food

The historic 1895 **Little Italy** (111 S. Main St., 585/374-6641, www.napleslittleitaly. info, Tues.-Sat. 4pm-9pm, Sun. 4pm-8pm, $17) specializes in traditional Italian fare. On Saturdays, live music is often presented in the hotel's rathskeller downstairs.

Brew & Brats (6461 Rte. 64, 585/374-2870, www.brewandbrats.com, Fri.-Sun. noon-9pm, $7) specializes in local craft brews and nearly 10 kinds of bratwurst. Non-drinkers can enjoy non-alcoholic slushies made of locally-made grape juice or root beer. Saturday nights feature live music.

Rochester

Rochester (pop. 210,532) straddles the Genesee River gorge just south of Lake Ontario and north of the Erie Canal. New York's third-largest city, Rochester has traditionally been known for its corporate and high-tech industries, with Eastman Kodak, Xerox, and Bausch & Lomb being the biggest. Many major educational and cultural institutions are based here as well, including the Eastman School of Music, Rochester Philharmonic, National Museum of Play at The Strong, and International Museum of Photography at the George Eastman House.

Established in 1803, Rochester became America's first boomtown with the opening of the Erie Canal, increasing its population 13-fold between 1825 and 1845. During the mid-1800s, Rochester was a hotbed of radical thought and social activism. Frederick Douglass, the escaped slave and abolitionist, settled in Rochester in 1847 and published his newspaper, *The Northern Star,* here for 17 years. One of his close associates was Susan B. Anthony, who was arrested in 1872 for daring to vote in a national election.

In 1881, a quiet young bank clerk named George Eastman patented and produced the world's first rollable film, an invention that changed Rochester forever. By the turn of the century, Eastman Kodak was Rochester's largest employer, and Eastman was a generous philanthropist. During his lifetime, he gave away over $100 million (more than $1 billion in today's economy) mainly to schools, parks, the University of Rochester, and local hospitals. "I want to make Rochester the best city in which to live and work." He succeeded: For much of

the 20th century, Rochester was famed for its prosperity.

In more recent decades, the city has been forced to reinvent itself. As Eastman Kodak and other major employers have downsized or shuttered completely, laying off thousands of employees, Rochester's population has learned to take nothing for granted. The city has traded its identity as a company town for one characterized by local businesses and smaller firms. Rochester today is home to dozens of thriving but relatively unknown computer software, telecommunications, and medical equipment companies. Downtown Rochester is experiencing something of a renaissance, and many of the city's suburbs remain prosperous.

Famous Rochesterians include musicians Cab Calloway, Mitch Miller, and Chuck Mangione. Jamaican-born Garth Fagan, the dancer, choreographer, and theater director best known for his choreography of the Broadway hit *The Lion King,* has lived in Rochester since 1970 and continues to headquarter his world-renowned eponymous dance troupe in the city.

Orientation

Downtown Rochester is encircled by I-490, sometimes called the Inner Loop. Main Street runs east-west through the center of downtown, flanked by a mix of historic buildings and modern glass-sheathed skyscrapers. Clinton Avenue runs north-south. At the corner of Main Street and Clinton Avenue sprawls the 1962 **Midtown Plaza,** the oldest downtown shopping mall in the country. At the corner of Main Street and South Avenue stand the **Rochester Riverside**

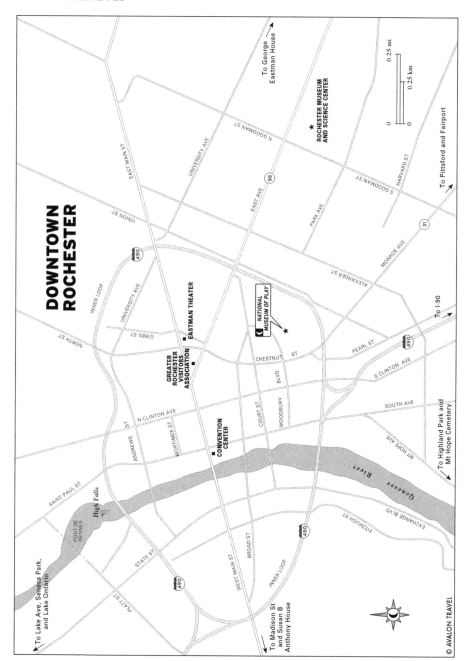

DOWNTOWN ROCHESTER

To George Eastman House

ROCHESTER MUSEUM AND SCIENCE CENTER

To Pittsford and Fairport

EAST MAIN ST

UNIVERSITY AVE

N GOODMAN ST

EAST AVE

96

UNION ST

PARK AVE

S GOODMAN ST

HARVARD ST

MONROE AVE

31

490

INNER LOOP

UNIVERSITY AVE

ALEXANDER ST

EASTMAN THEATER

NORTH ST

GIBBS ST

GREATER ROCHESTER VISITORS ASSOCIATION

NATIONAL MUSEUM OF PLAY

CHESTNUT ST

PEARL ST

To I-90

490

BLVD

S CLINTON AVE

N CLINTON AVE

COURT ST

WOODBURY

SOUTH AVE

To Highland Park and Mt Hope Cemetery

ST

MORTIMER ST

ANDREWS

CONVENTION CENTER

MT HOPE AVE

SAINT PAUL ST

Genesee River

EXCHANGE BLVD

High Falls

PONT DE RENNES

FITZHUGH ST

490

STATE ST

490

PLATT ST

WEST MAIN ST

BROAD ST

INNER LOOP

To Lake Ave, Seneca Park, and Lake Ontario

To Madison St and Susan B Anthony House

0.25 mi

0.25 km

0

0

© AVALON TRAVEL

Convention Center. Just west of South Street is the Genesee River. Graceful **Eastman Theatre,** with its rounded facade, is tucked onto Gibbs Street near Main Street, while the stunning Art Deco **Times Square Building** towers one block off Main Street at the intersection of Exchange Boulevard and Broad Street.

Major thoroughfares fanning out from I-490 include East Avenue, Park Avenue, Monroe Avenue (Route 31), and Mt. Hope Avenue (Route 15). I-90 runs just south of the city. Lake Ontario lies about eight miles north of the downtown.

The genteel southeastern quadrant of Rochester boasts four major museums, the University of Rochester, Mount Hope Cemetery, and Highland Park. Expansive **East Avenue,** peppered with stately mansions, gardens, and churches, runs through its center. Parallel to East Avenue runs **Park Avenue,** known for its classy boutiques, restaurants, and outdoor cafés. South of Park Avenue lies **Monroe Avenue,** a major commercial artery that's also one of the city's more eclectic neighborhoods. It's a haven for students, artists, performers, and activists. Most of the activity is centered between I-490 and Goodman Street.

You'll find several parking garages downtown, on or just off Main Street. Street parking is generally available elsewhere in the city. Downtown sights are within walking distance of each other and the major museums in southeast Rochester.

SIGHTS
High Falls and Brown's Race
Walk a few blocks north of Main Street and you'll see an enormous gaping gorge that rips right through the heart of the city, providing spectacular views. Brown's Race sits at the edge of wide, semi-circular, 96-foot-high High Falls. Cupping the falls to both sides, but especially to the east, are jagged brown walls streaked with dull red. A **pedestrian bridge** crosses the river just south of the falls.

Brown's Race is made up of four interconnected brick buildings that once contained water-powered mills. Extensively renovated in the early 1990s, it now features shops and restaurants. The word "race" refers to the diverted raceways that once harnessed the power of the falls.

◖ National Museum of Play
The **National Museum of Play** (1 Manhattan Sq., 585/263-2700, www.museumofplay.org, Mon.-Thurs. 10am-5pm, Fri.-Sat. 10am-8pm, Sun. noon-5pm, children over 2 and adults $13, children under 2 free) is one of the largest children's museums in the country, with 150,000 square feet of exhibits. The National Toy Hall of Fame features new and historic versions of classic toys. Main interactive exhibits include Sesame Street, a kid-sized supermarket, and a 1918 carousel.

Before her death in 1969, the museum's founder, Margaret Woodbury Strong, the daughter of wealthy parents, had amassed more than 300,000 objects, some of which she began collecting as a child. Often, during her family's many trips abroad, she was given a large shopping bag at the start of each day and told she could shop until she filled it.

Strong's many passions included fans, parasols, Asian artifacts and art, dolls, dollhouses, miniatures, toys, marbles, canes, paperweights, glass, pottery, samplers, figurines, kitchen equipment, and costumes. Her doll collection, numbering 27,000, is especially impressive. Many of these items remain on display.

Memorial Art Gallery
Connected with the University of Rochester, **Memorial Art Gallery** (500 University Ave., 585/276-8900, www.mag.rochester.edu, Wed.-Sun. 11am-5pm, Thurs. 11am-9pm, adults $12, seniors $8, students and children 6-18 $5) is a small gem, containing a little bit of everything, from pre-Columbian sculpture and ancient Chinese ceramics to American folk art and late-20th-century painting. The gallery owns more than 9,500 objects in all, spanning 5,000 years. A dozen or so temporary exhibitions are staged each year. In the center of the gallery is an enclosed, sky-lit sculpture garden

filled with works by Henry Moore and Albert Paley, a Rochesterian.

Rochester Museum and Science Center

Like many other top science museums, **Rochester Museum and Science Center** (657 East Ave., 585/271-4320, www.rmsc.org, Mon.-Sat. 9am-5pm, Sun. 11am-5pm, adults $13, seniors and students $12, children 3-18 $11) houses plenty of fossils, dioramas, exhibits on flora and fauna, and prehistoric beasts.

What makes the place really unusual, however, is **At the Western Door,** a powerful exhibit about the Seneca Nation. The exhibit examines Seneca life from pre-European contact in the 1550s to the present. Separate sections, brimming with artifacts, focus on such subjects as the fur trade, the Iroquois Confederacy, the Sullivan campaign, and the sad history of broken treaties. As late as 1960, the Allegheny Senecas lost one-third of their reservation when it was flooded to create Kinzua Dam.

State-of-the-art **Strasenburgh Planetarium** (sky shows $6-7) is also at the museum.

George Eastman House

Just east of the Rochester Museum and Science Center is the grand, 50-room **George Eastman House** (900 East Ave., 585/271-3361, www. eastmanhouse.org, Tues.-Sat. 10am-5pm, Sun. 11am-5pm, adults $12, seniors $10, students $5, children 12 and under free), where Eastman Kodak founder George Eastman lived alone with his mother for much of his life. The Georgian mansion contains all the finest furnishings of its day, including Persian rugs, oil paintings, and carved mahogany furniture polished to a high gleam. But what makes the place interesting is the information and ephemera related to Eastman himself.

Born in 1854, Eastman left school at age 13 to help support his family. He worked first as a messenger boy, earning $3 a week, then as an accountant. He began taking photographs at age 23 while on vacation and started searching for an easier way to develop negatives. He

spent three years experimenting in his mother's kitchen. By 1880, Eastman had invented a dry plate coating machine, the genesis of his Eastman Kodak Company.

Eastman's passions included music, fresh flowers, wild game hunting, and philanthropy. One year, he gave a free camera to every child in America who was turning 13. Then, at age 78, suffering from an irreversible spinal disease, he committed suicide in his bedroom. His suicide note read: "To my friends; My work is done—why wait?"

Adjoining the mansion is the **International Museum of Photography,** a modern museum holding a fascinating collection of antique cameras and photographic equipment, along with two theaters and four galleries. First-rate exhibits by artists such as Ansel Adams and Henri Cartier-Bresson are presented.

Stone-Tolan House Museum

Continuing to the far eastern end of East Avenue, you'll come to the oldest structure in Rochester, the 1792 **Stone-Tolan House Museum** (2370 East Ave., 585/546-7029, www.landmarksociety.org, Mar.-Dec. Fri.-Sat. noon-3pm, adults $5, children $2). A handsome, rustic building with wide floorboards, large fireplaces, and an orchard out back, the house was once both the Stone family home and a popular tavern. It is now owned by the Landmark Society of Western New York.

Highland Park

In 1888, Frederick Law Olmsted designed Highland Park, a planned arboretum bounded by Mt. Hope, Highland, and Elm Avenues and Goodman Street. One of the city's biggest celebrations, the Lilac Festival, takes place here every May, when the park's 1,200 lilac bushes bloom.

But lilacs are just the beginning. From early spring through late fall, Highland offers a riotous delight of Japanese maples, sweet-smelling magnolias, dazzling spring bulbs, delicate wildflowers, and 700 varieties of rhododendrons, azaleas, and mountain laurel.

In the center of the park reigns the 1911

Lamberton Conservatory (180 Reservoir Ave., 585/753-7270, daily 10am-4pm, adults $3, seniors and children $2). A tropical forest grows under the main dome, while other rooms contain orchid collections, banana trees, cacti, and house plants. Across from the conservatory is the 1898 **Frederick Douglass statue,** the first public statue erected to honor an African American.

Mount Hope Cemetery

From the corner of Mt. Hope and Elmwood Avenues extends extravagant **Mount Hope Cemetery** (entrance at 1133 Mt. Hope Ave.), a landscaped oasis of green strewn with knobby hills, ancient trees, marble tombs, and elaborate mausoleums. One of the oldest cemeteries in the country, established in 1838, Mt. Hope contains the graves of every Rochesterian who was anyone, including Frederick Douglass and Susan B. Anthony.

An 1874 neo-Romanesque gatehouse marks the cemetery entrance, while just inside are a Gothic chapel and a white Moorish gazebo. The Douglass grave is off East Avenue near the northern end of the cemetery; the Anthony grave is off Indian Trail Avenue at the far northern end.

Maps to the cemetery are available at the Rochester Convention and Visitors Bureau. **Friends of Mt. Hope Cemetery** (585/461-3494, www.fomh.org) offers guided walking tours on Saturdays in the spring, summer, and fall.

Susan B. Anthony House

In a quiet, somewhat run-down neighborhood west of downtown stands the narrow, red-brick **Susan B. Anthony House** (17 Madison St., off W. Main St., 585/235-6124, www.susanbanthonyhouse.org, Tues.-Sun. 11am-5pm, adults $10, seniors $8, students and children $5) that once belonged to the women's rights advocate. Simply furnished in the style of the late 1800s, the house contains much Anthony memorabilia, including her typewriters, clothes, letters, photos, and stuffed Victorian furniture.

Anthony, born in Massachusetts in 1820, lived in this house from 1866 until her death in 1906. It was here where she was arrested for voting in 1872, and here that she met and planned with fellow reformers Elizabeth Cady Stanton and Frederick Douglass. Together with Elizabeth Cady Stanton and Matilda Gage, Anthony wrote her *History of Woman Suffrage* in the third-floor attic, a wonderful hideaway now once again strewn with her books and papers.

Seneca Park Zoo

North of the downtown, along the Genesee River, runs the long, skinny **Seneca Park Zoo** (2222 St. Paul St., 585/336-7200, www.senecaparkzoo.org, Nov. 1-Mar. 31 daily 10am-3pm, Apr. 1-Oct. 31 daily 10am-4pm, rates vary seasonally, adults $9-11, seniors $8-10, children 3-11 $6-8). About 500 animals from nearly 200 species live in the zoo, including polar bears, a Siberian tiger, and reindeer. Don't miss the aviary, where brightly colored tropical birds fly about freely. Younger kids will enjoy the barnyard petting area.

Ontario Beach Park

When in downtown Rochester, it's easy to forget that Lake Ontario is less than 15 minutes away. But indeed, north of the city along Lake Avenue, you'll soon find a land of wide open spaces, beaches, and parks.

Just before reaching the lake, you'll pass the 1822 **Charlotte-Genesee Lighthouse** (70 Lighthouse St., 585/621-6179, www.geneseelighthouse.org, hours vary seasonally, adults $3, children under 17 free), now a small museum with exhibits tracing the history of lighthouses and lake transportation. Originally, the lighthouse stood on the lakeshore, but sand deposits have moved it inland.

Ontario Beach Park (Lake and Beach Aves., 585/753-5887) is a 0.5-mile-long beach with an aging Art Deco bathhouse and weathered fishing pier illuminated on summer nights. Around the turn of the century, the park was the "Coney Island of the West," attracting tens of thousands of Rochesterians to its elephant shows, water slides, and beachfront hotels. Harking back to those heady days is the park's still-operating 1905 **Dentzel menagerie carousel,** one of the oldest carousels in the United States. Stop by the locally famous **Abbott's Custard** (www.abbottscustard.com), at the park's entrance, for sweet, creamy ice-cream.

Seabreeze Amusement Park

From Ontario Beach Park, travel east about five miles along Lake Shore Boulevard to reach **Seabreeze Amusement Park** (4600 Culver Rd., 585/323-1900, www.seabreeze.com, June-Aug. daily 11am-8pm, May weekends). First established in 1879, the park has over 75 rides and attractions, including a water park. It's also the home of the oldest continuously operating roller coaster in the United States, the **Jack Rabbit,** which opened in 1920.

An unlimited Ride & Slide Pass is $27.99 for those 48 inches and taller and $22.99 for those under 48 inches. A Spectator Pass allows access to the grounds, but no rides, and costs $11.99. Tickets are several dollars cheaper if bought in advance on the park's website.

RECREATION

The 49-passenger *Sam Patch* (585/662-5748, www.samandmary.org, May-Oct.), a replica packet boat, offers sightseeing and specialty cruises, as does the historic wooden boat, *Mary Jemison.*

ENTERTAINMENT

Classical Music

The renowned **Rochester Philharmonic Orchestra** (585/454-7311, www.rpo.org) performs at the Eastman Theatre October-May. One of the world's premier music schools, **Eastman School of Music** (26 Gibbs St., 585/274-1000, www.esm.rochester.edu) stages over 700 performances annually by students, faculty, and guest artists. **Hochstein School of Music and Dance** (50 N. Plymouth Ave., 585/454-4596, www.hochstein.org) hosts the Rochester Chamber Orchestra and classical music concerts.

Theater

Rochester's resident professional theater, **Geva Theatre** (75 Woodbury Blvd., 585/232-4382, www.gevatheatre.org) stages nearly a dozen productions annually. It's housed in a historic brick-and-limestone building that was once the Naval Armory. **Downstairs Cabaret Theatre** (20 Windsor St., 585/325-4370, www.downstairscabaret.org) produces popular comedies and musicals.

Rochester Broadway Theatre League (885 Main St., 585/325-7760, www.rbtl.org) presents touring Broadway shows and concerts, while **Rochester Contemporary Art Center** (137 East Ave., 585/461-2222, www.rochestercontemporary.org) is the place to go for performance art and avant-garde theater.

Live Music and Nightlife

The best music listings are published by *City Newspaper* (www.rochestercitynewspaper.com), a free alternative weekly. One of the biggest and most active music clubs in the city is **Water Street Music Hall** (204 N. Water St., 585/325-5600, www.waterstreetmusic.com). Regional and national acts play blues, rock, funk, and industrial.

California Brew Haus (402 W. Ridge Rd., 585/621-1480) presents a good dose of Southern rock in a space that is the longest, continuously operated rock and roll bar in the city.

Rochester International Jazz Festival (downtown Rochester, www.rochesterjazz.com) is a massive event each June, held over the course of more than a week, featuring more than 300 concerts and 1,200 performers in nearly 20 different venues, all within walking distance of downtown's East End Cultural District. Options to attend include approximately 80 free performances, 40 headliner shows, over 180 club pass concerts, and dozens of late-night, no-cover charge jam sessions.

ACCOMMODATIONS

There are a handful of great places to stay, all in downtown Rochester. In a city of nearly all chain hotels, **Inn on Broadway** (26 Broadway, 585/232-3595, www.innonbroadway.com,

$169-199) is a boutique hotel housed in the historic 1929 University Club of Rochester. Luxury rooms include polished hardwood floors and natural stone bathrooms with extra touches like multi-headed showers, whirlpool tubs, Keurig coffeemakers, and gas fireplaces. Complimentary continental breakfast is served in elegant Tournedos, a restaurant whose lunch and dinner menus feature in-house dry-aged beef, seafood flown in daily from Hawaii, and a wine list with over 550 selections.

The **East Avenue Inn & Suites** (384 East Ave., 585/325-5010, www.eastaveinn.com, $129-169), fresh off a 2012-2013 renovation, transformed from a cheap and basic hotel to a boutique property where Wi-Fi, parking, and breakfast are all free.

One of the loveliest bed-and-breakfasts in Rochester is **Dartmouth House** (215 Dartmouth St., 585/271-7872, www.dartmouthhouse.com, $109-209), a spacious English Tudor home with a fireplace, window seats, very knowledgeable hosts, and four guest rooms equipped with private baths. The bed-and-breakfast is within easy walking distance of several museums and many cafés and shops.

Another good bed-and-breakfast choice is romantic **Edward Harris House Inn** (35 Argyle St., 585/473-9752, www.edwardharrishouse.com, $169-189), with nice touches like fresh flowers, robes and towel warmers, sunflower showerheads, all organic and natural breakfasts, and welcome snack baskets.

Just outside Rochester, **Woodcliff Hotel and Spa** (199 Woodcliff Dr., Fairport, 585/381-4000, www.woodcliffhotelspa.com, $156-540), is a perfect home base for exploring the surrounding area's attractions, including small canal towns like Fairport. The room decor runs the gamut from Art Deco to Southwestern to Asian. The expansive property has spa and a 9-hole golf course, as well as an on-site restaurant.

FOOD

For a quick lunch, visit **DiBella's Old Fashioned Submarines** (620 Jefferson Rd., 585/475-1831, www.dibellas.com, Mon.-Sat. 10am-9pm, Sun. 11am-7pm, $10), serving hot and cold subs on hand-shaped rolls since 1918. Another good lunch spot is **Orange Glory Café** (240 East Ave., 585/232-7340, www.orangeglorycafe.com, Mon.-Fri. 11am-3pm, $8), which offers tasty homemade organic dishes, gourmet sandwiches, and cookies. Head to this little eatery early for the best selection.

In the heart of downtown, **Dinosaur Bar-B-Que** (99 Court St., 585/325-7090, www.dinosaurbarbque.com, Mon.-Wed. 11am-11pm, Thurs. 11am-midnight, Fri.-Sat. 11am-1am, Sun. noon-10pm, $12) offers great ribs and Cajun food, along with live blues on weekends. Romantic **Tapas 177 Lounge** (177 St. Paul St., 585/262-2090, www.tapas177.com, $16) is a very popular spot, serving an eclectic menu by candlelight. The lounge also features a wide variety of martinis, salsa lessons, and live music on the weekends.

The spirits of generations of brewers permeate the cavernous **Genesee Brew House** (25 Cataract St., 585/263-9200, www.geneseebeer.com, 11am-9pm Mon.-Wed., 11am-10pm Thurs.-Sat., noon-9:00pm Sun.), one of the country's oldest, continuously operating breweries. Expect typical American brew pub fare like burgers and wings, served alongside Genesee's own brews. A guest tap features other local beers.

Nestled into the East End entertainment district is popular **2 Vine** (24 Winthrop St., 585/454-6020, www.2vine.com, Mon.-Thurs. 11:30am-10pm, Fri. 11:30am-11pm, Sat. 5pm-11pm, $26), serving lots of fresh seafood flown in daily, fresh local produce, and homemade pastries.

For a simple salad or tofu burger, step into no-frills **Aladdin's Natural Eatery** (646 Monroe Ave., 585/442-5000, www.myaladdins.com, $8). On Clinton Avenue, parallel to Monroe, is **Highland Park Diner** (960 S. Clinton Ave., 585/461-5040, www.highland-park-diner.com, Mon.-Thurs. and Sat. 7am-9pm, Fri. 7am-10pm, Sun. 7am-8pm, $10), a classic 1948 Art Deco Orleans diner.

On Jefferson Road, you'll find **Raj Mahal**

(368 Jefferson Rd., 585/730-7360, www.rajma-halrestaurant.com, $14), known for its tandoori and vegetarian dishes and fresh breads.

VICINITY OF ROCHESTER
Pittsford
To the immediate southeast of the city, the canal town of Pittsford offers unique shops and cafés, some inhabiting historic buildings. The town's **Lock 32** (585/328-3960, www.genesee-waterways.org, hours and prices vary season-ally) offers whitewater kayaking in the spillway. Live music also rocks the locks, with a **Summer Concert Series** (Port of Pittsford Park, 22 N. Main Street, www.townofpittsford.org, free), **Positively Pittsford** (Main St. and Church St., www.townofpittsford.org, free), and **Pittsford Celebrates** (www.townofpittsford.org, free), all filled with family entertainment and the occasional fireworks display.

Bushnell's Basin, a charming spot to dock just outside of the village, is home to one of Rochester's landmark restaurants, **Richardson's Canal House** (1474 Marsh Rd., 585/248-5000, www.richardsoncanalhouse.net, Mon.-Sat. 5pm-10pm, $28), a restored 1818 Erie Canal tavern with its own secluded garden. Elegant and highly acclaimed, the restaurant serves French country and American regional fare by candlelight.

Along the banks of the canal, **Coal Tower** (9 Schoen Pl., 585/381-7866, www.villagecoal-tower.com, hours vary seasonally) serves burgers and sandwiches.

Macedon
Macedon's **Mid-Lakes Erie Macedon Landing** is the home marina to **Mid-Lakes Navigation** (315/685-8500, www.midlakesnav.com), where you can learn to drive one of the gleaming wooden canal boats that await visitors who come to relive a bit of history. These simple-to-pilot boats can be driven by anyone with a few lessons.

Nearby **Long Acre Farms** (1342 Eddy Rd., 315/986-4202, www.longacrefarms.com), a family farm with a Scandinavian jumping pillow (for all ages), gemstone panning, and the Amazing Maize Maze, attracts visitors. The town's annual, mid-September **Lumberjack Festival** (Macedon Center Fireman's Field, Rte. 31 and Canandaigua Rd., 315/986-3732, www.macedoncenter-fire.org) lets even amateurs unleash their inner Paul Bunyan with log rolling and team greased pole climbing.

Fairport
The bustling, canal-side community of Fairport can be explored with bicycle rentals from **RV&E** (40 N. Main St., 585/388-1350, www.rvebike.com) or kayak rentals from **Erie Canal Boat Company** (7 Lift Bridge Ln., 585/748-2628, www.eriecanalboatcompany.com). For a more in depth look at life on the canal, join an overnight excursion, which includes kayak rental, food, and an overnight campsite with sleeping gear. Paddling adventures with itineraries for up to 10 days are also available.

With any luck, a boater will need the **Lift Bridge** triggered, the only one of its kind on the canal system. With no angle the same, the irregularly constructed bridge once largely stayed raised in a crooked slant at its top 15-foot height to allow for the high volume of traffic on the canal below. A pedestrian bridge was created to accommodate foot traffic in this raised position. Current times see more road traffic, so the opposite is true and the bridge is raised from its usual six-foot-above-the-water level only when a boat needs to pass.

Red Bird Market (130 Village Landing, 585/377-5050, www.redbirdmarket.com) is a good morning pre-paddle pit stop for baked goods and coffee. Afternoon cool downs can be had at **Donnelly's Public House** (1 Water St., 585/377-5450, www.donnellysph.com), an excellent pub with 33 taps and good pub food.

GENESEE COUNTRY VILLAGE AND MUSEUM

Twenty miles southwest of Rochester, world-class **Genesee Country Village and Museum** (1410 Flint Hill Rd., Mumford, 585/538-6822, www.gcv.org, hours vary seasonally, adults $15.50, seniors and students $12.50, children ages 4-16 $9.50) consists of more than 40 meticulously restored and furnished 19th-century buildings laid out around a village square, depicting life of three different historic periods. Among the buildings are an early land office, two-story log cabin, flytier's shop, octagonal house, Greek Revival mansion, Italianate mansion, bookshop, small-scale farm, blacksmith's shop, doctor's office, and pharmacy. Gravel walkways lead between the buildings; guides in period dress cook, spin, weave, and demonstrate other folk arts of the pre-industrial age.

Near the entrance are a Carriage Museum and **The John L. Wehle Art Gallery,** which houses a world-class collection of wildlife and sporting art spanning four centuries of work by such artists as Audubon and Remington. An extensive renovation completed in 2012 also debuted a new exhibit: the Susan Greene Historic Clothing Collection, a remarkably intact representation of period clothing, unique for its pieces that represent both the working class (whose clothing was so well-worn that it rarely survived to be able to be exhibited) and the upper class.

Another delightful curiosity on the grounds is *The Intrepid,* a replica Civil War-era helium balloon. Its basket occasionally holds passengers, who soar up to 300 feet over the Genesee grounds.

An heirloom garden provides blooms and seeds to be used in the village. To the north is a 175-acre **Nature Center,** networked with three miles of hiking and nature trails.

Little Finger Lakes

West of the six major Finger Lakes extend what are known as the little Finger Lakes: Honeoye (pronounced Honey-oy), Canadice, Hemlock, and Conesus. Honeoye sports a village of the same name at its northern end, and Conesus—closest to Rochester—is crowded with summer homes. Canadice and Hemlock, which serve as reservoirs for Rochester, remain largely undeveloped and comprise Hemlock/Canadice State Forest. Set in deep, wooded valleys with no towns nearby, these two Finger Lakes are totally undeveloped. As a state forest, they and their surroundings will remain "forever green." Fishing, boating, and hiking can be enjoyed in the area.

HONEOYE

At the southwestern end of Honeoye lies the largely undeveloped **Harriet Hollister Spencer State Recreation Area** (Canadice Hill Rd./ Rte. 37, 585/335-8111, www.nysparks.com/ parks/164/details.aspx). Set on Canadice Hill, the park offers great views of the lake and, on a clear day, the Rochester skyline.

Another quirky stop outside Honeoye is the unusual **Wizard of Clay** (7851 Rte. 20A, Bloomfield, 585/229-2980, www.wizardofclay. com), where the Kozlowski potters use 100,000 pounds of clay each year, hand-throwing the family's functional creations. The workshop is open to tour and see each stage of the process, even that of the unique patented Bristoleaf collection, made by pressing locally collected leaves into the soft clay before firing, leaving the imprints to be glazed for a final vase or picture frame. A densely pinned map on the wall shows the hometowns of thousands of visitors.

Accommodations and Food

The area offers several good lodging options including **Little Lakes Inn and Healing Center** (4646 County Rd. 37, Honeoye,

585/229-5557, www.littlelakesinn.com, $135-165), an Italianate style inn with five suites and an on-site "healing center," which offers traditional spa treatments alongside more mystical-sounding therapies.

Abner Adams House (2 Howard Ave., Bloomfield, 585/657-4681, www.abneradamshouse.com, $159-179) is a sturdy brick home built in 1810, featuring high ceilings and wood floors. All three guest rooms have fireplaces.

The Holloway House (29 State St., Bloomfield, 585/657-7120, www.thehollowayhouse.com, Tues.-Fri. 11:30am-2pm and 5pm-9pm, Sat. 5pm-9pm, Sun. 11:30am-7:30pm) is a fine dining restaurant located in a colonial home built in 1808. American favorites include roast duck and broiled lamb chops.

LETCHWORTH STATE PARK

Along the Genesee River at the far western edge of the Finger Lakes plunges one of the most magnificent sights in the state: 17-mile-long Letchworth Gorge, now part of **Letchworth State Park** (1 Letchworth State Park, Castile, 585/493-3600, camping reservations 800/456-2267, www.nysparks.com/parks/79, daily 6am-11pm, $8 parking). Dubbed the "Grand Canyon of the East," the gorge is flanked by dark gray cliffs rising nearly 600 feet. Dense, thicketed forest grows all around and at the center of it all sparkle three thundering waterfalls. Excellent hiking and snowshoeing are available through the wild terrain.

Much of the Letchworth Gorge was purchased by industrialist William P. Letchworth in 1859. A conservationist and humanitarian, Letchworth bought the gorge both for his own personal use and to save the falls from becoming Rochester's hydroelectric plant. Before his death in 1910, he deeded the gorge to the people of New York to be used as a permanent park.

One main road runs through the park alongside the gorge, affording scenic views. Recreational facilities include over 25 hiking trails ranging from 0.5 to 7 miles in length, two swimming pools, 82 cabins, and a 270-site campground.

The park can be entered from Mt. Morris (off Rte. 36), Portageville (off Rtes. 19A or 436), or Castile (off Rte. 19A); Portageville entrances are closed in winter.

Letchworth Museum

At the southern end of the park stands the rambling **Letchworth Museum** (585/493-2760, May-Oct. daily 10am-5pm) with exhibits on the Seneca, William Letchworth, and the gorge's natural history. Note especially the exhibits relating to Mary Jemison, the "white woman of the Genesee."

The daughter of Irish immigrants, Jemison was taken prisoner by the Seneca at the age of 15 and lived the rest of her life among them. She married first a Delaware warrior and then, following his death, a Seneca chief; she bore seven children, and became a Seneca leader in her own right. Under the Big Tree Treaty of 1797, she was granted close to 18,000 acres along the Genesee River. Eventually, however, Jemison was moved to the Buffalo Creek Reservation with the rest of her people, where she died at the age of 91.

Letchworth moved Jemison's remains to the gorge in 1910 when her grave was in danger of being destroyed, and today, the **Mary Jemison Grave** stands on a hill behind the museum. Also on the hill is the **Council House** in which the last Iroquois council on the Genesee River was held on October 1, 1872. In attendance were the grandchildren of Red Jacket, Joseph Brant, and Mary Jemison; and William Letchworth and Millard Fillmore.

Accommodations and Food

At the southern end of the park, across from the Letchworth Museum is the **Glen Iris Inn** (inside Letchworth State Park, 585/493-2622, www.glenirisinn.com, breakfast, lunch, and dinner, $18), a favorite lunch spot. The inn's bustling restaurant, flanked by picture windows, specializes in gourmet salads prepared tableside, seafood, and veal. The stately, yellow-and-white **⟨ Glen Iris Inn** (inside Letchworth State Park, 585/493-2622, www.glenirisinn.com, $95-120) sits in a large flat field overlooking the 107-foot Middle Falls. Once the home of William Letchworth, the Victorian mansion is now a modernized inn with 16 comfortable guest rooms, a library with a good collection of regional books, and a gift shop.

For a serene, scenic splurge, check availability for the signature **Cherry Suite at the Glen Iris Inn** (inside Letchworth State Park, 585/493-2622, www.glenirisinn.com, $210), which features patterned hardwood floors, a whirlpool tub, and a balcony overlooking the incredible middle falls. The balcony of the Cherry Suite, perched above the glass-walled restaurant, is a coveted spot of passersby. Four-bedroom **The Stone House** (585/493-2622, $350 for up to 8 people) is another option rented by Letchworth State Park, situated across from Inspiration Point overlook.

The Thousand Islands

An hour or two from the northeastern part of the Finger Lakes is the Thousand Islands-Seaway region, accessible by I-81. In point of fact, there are 1,864 islands here, ranging in size from a few square feet to 22 miles long. Some support nothing more than a lone tree; one is home to Boldt Castle, a haunting Gothic presence near Alexandria Bay that is the region's premier visitor attraction.

Though the term "Thousand Islands" is often used to describe the large area reaching from Oswego in the south to Akwesasne in the north to Adirondack Park in the east, the islands themselves are clustered only in the center, between Cape Vincent and Alexandria Bay. Much of the rest of the region supports farms or endless unbroken acres of low-growing forests, rivers, and lakes.

Prior to the arrival of Europeans, the Thousand Islands were inhabited by the Iroquois, who called the region Manitonna, or Garden of the Great Spirit. The first white man to enter the region was Jacques Cartier, who sailed down the St. Lawrence in 1635 and allegedly exclaimed, *"Les milles isles!"* Later, the region bore the brunt of much of the War of 1812. Handsome stone fortifications still stand in Sackets Harbor and Oswego, where major battles were fought. The wealthy discovered the beauty of the Thousand Islands in the 1870s and soon built magnificent summer homes on private islands. Grand hotels went up on the shore as well, and huge steamboats plied the waters.

All this opulence ended with the Depression, but evidence of it remains.

Most of the Thousand Islands' attractions lie along the Seaway Trail, which hugs the shores of the St. Lawrence and Lake Ontario. From the trail, views of the river and its bypassing boat traffic are outstanding. Enormous tankers and cargo vessels slide by, on their way between the Atlantic Ocean and the Great Lakes. The 1959 completion of the St. Lawrence Seaway—a series of connecting channels and locks—turned the river into the longest navigable inland water passage in the world. It stretches over 2,300 miles.

New York and Canada share the islands. Canada's oldest national park east of the Rockies, Thousand Islands National Park, is here, where the Canadian Shield mountain range connects across the river with New York's Adirondack Mountains. As a result, the region attracts as many Canadian visitors as American visitors. The Thousand Islands International Bridge (an extension of I-81) crosses over the St. Lawrence River near Alexandria Bay; the Prescott-Ogdensburg Bridge connects the two cities, and the Seaway International Bridge spans the river near Massena.

OSWEGO

The small city of Oswego (pop. 18,142) sits at the southwestern end of the region, just north of the Finger Lakes. Straddling the mouth of the Oswego River and overlooking Lake Ontario, Oswego operated as an important fort

THE SEAWAY TRAIL

The Seaway Trail is a 518-mile scenic highway that parallels New York's northern coastline along the St. Lawrence River, Lake Ontario, the Niagara River, and Lake Erie. Marked by green-and-white route markers, as well as brown-and-white War of 1812 signs, it is the longest national recreational trail in the United States.

In the Thousand Islands region, the Seaway Trail runs from Oswego in the south to Akwesasne in the north along Routes 104, 3, 180, 12 E, and 37. More parks and beaches are located along this section of the trail than anywhere else in New York State. In total, the Thousand Islands region boasts 45 New York and Canadian state parks; two of the largest are Wellesley Island and Robert Moses.

Seaway Trail, Inc. (401 W. Main St., Sackets Harbor, 315/646-1000, www.seawaytrail.com) publishes a free annual magazine, available in most regional tourism offices, and helpful touring guides. Among them are *Seaway Trail Bicycling,* which outlines some of the region's excellent bike routes, and *Seaway Trail Lighthouses.* Their website is a rich resource, with detailed maps available for download.

and trading post throughout the 1700s. During the American Revolution, Oswego served as a haven for Loyalists fleeing the Mohawk Valley, and remained in British hands until 1796. Named the first freshwater port in the United States in 1799, Oswego protected the supply route to the naval base at nearby Sackets Harbor during the War of 1812.

Today, Oswego continues to function as a Great Lakes port and is a major sport-fishing center.

Fort Ontario State Historic Site

Fort Ontario State Historic Site (1 E. 4th St., 315/343-4711, www.nysparks.com/historic-sites/20, July 1-Sept. 2 daily 10am-4:30pm, hours vary off-season, adults $4, seniors and students $3, children 12 and under free) continues to stand sentinel over Lake Ontario, nearly 200 years after it was built. Originally built by the British in 1755, the site was attacked and rebuilt four times, with the present-day fort constructed between 1839 and 1844.

During World War II, Fort Ontario served as a sort of emergency refugee center/internment camp for victims of the Holocaust. The only one of its kind for European refugees in the country, the center invited 874 Jews and 73 Catholics to relocate here, but upon arrival, the refugees were placed in a fenced-in compound

and told not to leave. The shocked refugees were interned for a total of 18 months.

Today, Fort Ontario has been restored to its 1867-72 appearance. Costumed guides interpret the lives of soldiers and civilians who once lived here.

H. Lee White Marine Museum

The delightful **H. Lee White Marine Museum** (1 W. 1st St. at West First St. Pier, 315/342-0480, www.hleewhitemarinemuseum.com, Sept.-June daily 1pm-5pm, July-Aug. daily 10am-5pm, adults $7, children 13-17 $3, children 12 and under free) is a sprawling, hodgepodge affair filled with everything from archaeological artifacts to mounted fish. One exhibit focuses on Lake Ontario shipwrecks; another on the city's once-thriving ship-building industry; a third on the legendary "monsters" of the lake; and a fourth on the region's strong abolitionist history. Most everything in the museum has been donated, which gives it a folksy appeal. Outside, a World War II tugboat and a derrick barge invite exploration.

Richardson-Bates House Museum

Built in the late 1860s, **Richardson-Bates House Museum** (135 E. 3rd St., 315/343-1342, www.rbhousemuseum.org, Apr.-Dec. Thurs.-Sat 1pm-5pm, Jan.-Mar. by appointment,

adults $5, seniors and students $3, children 6-12 $2, children under 6 free) is a regal Italianate mansion still equipped with 95 percent of its original furnishings. The five plush period rooms downstairs are arranged according to photographs taken around 1890, while upstairs, succinct exhibits explain the history of Oswego County. The museum is run by the Oswego County Historical Society.

Camping

Selkirk Shores State Park (7101 Rte. 3, 315/298-5737, reservations 800/456-2267, www.nysparks.com/parks/84) is on the lakeshore about 15 miles northeast of Oswego.

It has a beach, hiking trails, and a 148-site campground.

Food

The ever popular **Rudy's Lakeside Drive-in** (78 Rte. 89, 315/343-2671, www.rudyshot.com), a quarter-mile west of the State University of New York (SUNY) College at Oswego, has been serving up fish and chips and fried scallops and clams since 1946.

EN ROUTE TO SACKETS HARBOR

The **Seaway Trail** (Rte. 104 to Rte. 3) heads north out of Oswego to Selkirk Shores State

Park and the mouth of the Salmon River. Take a two-mile detour east on Route 13 along the river to reach the Salmon Capital of **Pulaski,** where almost everything caters to anglers.

Continue another five miles east on Route 13 to reach Altmar and the **New York State Salmon River Fish Hatchery** (2133 Rte. 22, Altmar, 315/298-5051, www.dec.ny.gov/outdoor/21663.html, Apr. 1-Nov. 30 daily 8:30am-3:30pm, free). Over three million fish are raised here each year, including chinook and coho salmon and brown, rainbow, and steelhead trout.

From the mouth of the Salmon River, Seaway Trail continues north along the shores of Lake Ontario. It bypasses several more parks and then bumps into deep blue **Henderson Harbor,** a perfectly shaped semicircle ringed with historic homes, vacation cottages, marinas, and ship-shape small boats.

About a mile southeast of Henderson Harbor is the hamlet of **Henderson,** where Confederate general Stonewall Jackson came for medical treatment for a stomach ailment before the Civil War. Part of his cure was to walk between the hamlet and the harbor daily.

SACKETS HARBOR

About 45 miles north of Oswego, or 8 miles west of Watertown, lies picturesque Sackets Harbor. Built on a bluff overlooking Lake Ontario, Sackets Harbor is peppered with handsome limestone buildings that date back to the early 1800s. Though now primarily a resort village, Sackets Harbor remains for the most part undiscovered, which helps account for its charm.

During the War of 1812, Sackets Harbor dominated American naval and military activity. A large fleet was constructed in its shipyard and thousands of soldiers were housed in the barracks built on its shores. Heavy fighting between British and American troops took place on the bluffs.

The former shipyard and adjoining battlefield is now Sackets Harbor's foremost visitor attraction. It is located at the end of a short Main Street lined with cheery shops, cafés,

and historic buildings; more historic buildings flank quiet, tree-shaded Broad Street.

Sackets Harbor Battlefield State Historic Site

The silent and all-but-deserted **Sackets Harbor Battlefield State Historic Site** (foot of Main and Washington Sts., 315/646-3634, www.sacketsharborbattlefield.org, grounds: daily dawn-dusk, buildings: May 24-June 30 Wed.-Sat. 10am-5pm, summer Mon.-Sat. 10am-5pm and Sun. 1pm-5pm, adults $3, seniors and students $2, children 12 and under free) was once the site of intense fighting between American and British troops. Monuments and plaques commemorating the events are strewn here and there, but for the most part, the battlefield remains an idyllic park, set atop a lush green bluff with glorious lake views. The **Battle of Sackets Harbor** is reenacted here every July.

Adjoining the battlefield is the partially restored Navy Yard, enclosed by a white picket fence. Built in the 1850s to replace the thriving shipyard once situated here, the yard contains a restored commandant's house and a museum showcasing exhibits on the War of 1812.

Madison Barracks

A mile or two east of the village center stand the former barracks, now known as **Madison Barracks** (85 Worth Rd., 315/646-3374, www.madisonbarracks.com), a converted complex holding apartments, restaurants, and a small inn. Visitors are welcome to explore the barracks' bucolic grounds, encompassing a parade ground, polo lawn, stone tower, officers' row, and military burial ground. Pick up walking-tour brochures in the management office just inside the main gate.

Augustus Sacket Mansion

Housed in the handsome 1803 **Augustus Sacket Mansion** (301 W. Main St.) is **Sackets Harbor Visitors Center** (315/646-2321, www.sacketsharborny.com, hours vary seasonally, free), which contains three rooms of exhibits and an informative introductory video on the area.

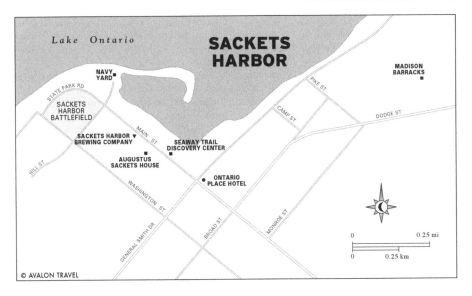

© AVALON TRAVEL

Seaway Trail Discovery Center

One block away from the visitors center is the **Seaway Trail Discovery Center** (401 W. Main St., 315/646-1000, www.seawaytrail.com, hours vary seasonally, adults $4, seniors $3, children $2), housed in the old Union Hotel, which was built in 1817. Here, you'll find nine rooms of exhibits and lots of free literature on the historic trail.

Accommodations

In the heart of the village, three-story **Ontario Place Hotel** (103 General Smith Dr., 315/646-8000, www.ontarioplacehotel.com, $90-165) offers 28 spacious rooms and 10 suites with whirlpool tubs.

Also in the center of town, **Jacob Brewster House B&B** (107 S. Broad St., 315/646-4663, www.jacobbrewsterbandb.com, $100-125) is a renovated 1815 New England-style Georgian house with four guest rooms. Each has a private bathroom, a fireplace, and free Wi-Fi.

Food

◖ **Sackets Harbor Brewing Company** (212 W. Main St., 315/646-2739, www. sacketsharborbrewpub.com, daily 11:30am-10pm, $25) is located in a refurbished railroad station in the heart of the village. Its historic location inspires the names of many of its brews, including War of 1812 Amber Ale and Grant's Golden Ale. On the dining room menu, find everything from fresh fish to pot pies; a pub menu is also available.

WATERTOWN

One of the few towns in the Thousand Islands whose population has increased in recent years (just over 27,000), Watertown is named for the numerous falls of the Black River. Its proximity to so many waterways was, in large part, responsible for its industrial prosperity, a prosperity that was so robust that the town was said to have the most millionaires—at least per capita—in the United States at the beginning of the 20th century. That wealth helped Watertown develop infrastructure and architecture that were particularly remarkable given its size. It is the smallest town to have a park designed by Frederick Law Olmsted, Thompson Park, which is the location of The New York State Zoo.

The New York State Zoo at Thompson Park

Nearly a century old, **The New York State Zoo** (1 Thompson Park, 315/782-6180, www. nyszoo.org, Mar.-Oct. daily 10am-5pm, Nov.-Feb. Sat.-Sun. 10am-4pm, adults $8, seniors $6, children 4-12 $5, children under 4 free) is a 32-acre park that focuses on species that are native to New York. Some of the species are common, while others are rare, threatened, or endangered. Among them, expect to see bears, eagles, and wolverines. The zoo has a particularly strong educational and family program, so if you're coming with kids, be sure to see what activities are planned during your visit.

Recreation

If you're keen to get out on the river to run the rapids, **Adirondack River Outfitters** (140 Newell St., 800/525-7238, www.aroadventures. com, May-Oct.) will take you on a Black River whitewater excursion. Expect 14 rapids ranging from Class II to Class IV.

Accommodations and Food

As Watertown's oldest restaurant, **The Crystal Restaurant** (87 Public Square, 315/782-9938, www.thecrystalrestaurant.com, Tues.-Sun. 7am-10pm) is an institution. Little has been done over the years to modernize the restaurant: the decor, the menu, and even the prices have refused to conform to trends. Service is generally excellent, which is one reason to visit. Another is the restaurant's contribution to cocktail culture: The Tom and Jerry, a Christmas holiday eggnog drink, wasn't invented here, but many locals claim it was perfected here. It's served only from Black Friday through New Year's Day.

Most lodging options in and immediately around Watertown are chain hotels, offering basic, reliable rooms and amenities.

CAPE VINCENT

Situated on a windswept spit of land at the mouth of the St. Lawrence River is Cape Vincent, "home of the gamey black bass" ("gamey" as in "feisty"). Cape Vincent has few tourist attractions, but it's a pretty village to drive through, with historic homes along Broadway.

The area's first European settlers were French, a fact that is celebrated every July on **French Heritage Day**. Real Street was once the location of "Cup and Saucer House," built in 1818 by Napoleon's chief of police, Count Real, in the hopes that the emperor could be rescued from the island of St. Helena. The building burned to the ground in 1867.

Sights

Cape Vincent Historical Museum (174 James St., 315/654-3094, July-Aug. Mon.-Sat. 10am-4pm, Sun. noon-4pm, free), in the heart of the village, showcases historical artifacts and a delightful collection of tiny figures created out of scrap metal by local farmer Richard Merchant. Not far from the museum is **New York State Department of Environmental Conservation's Research Station and Aquarium** (541 Broadway, 315/654-2147, May-Oct. daily 9am-4pm, free), housing several hundred local fish.

It's also worth driving out to the 1854 **Tibbetts Point Lighthouse** (33439 County Rte. 6, 315/654-3450, www.hiusa.org/cape-vincent), several miles west of the village on the very tip of the cape. The lighthouse is not open for touring—it's now a youth hostel—but the drive along the shore road (Route 6) is outstanding.

Horne's Ferry

Cape Vincent is the only community left in New York State with a ferry to Canada crossing the St. Lawrence River. **Horne's Ferry** (855/442-2262, www.hornesferry.com, $15 for car and driver, one-way, $2 per extra passenger) operates in May-October and it takes 10 minutes to cross the river on the ferry.

Accommodations and Food

Two blocks from the water, **Aubrey's Inn** (126 S. James St., 315/654-3754, www.aubreysinn. com, daily from 7am) offers inexpensive, generous portions at breakfast, lunch, and dinner.

For historic lodging, **Tibbetts Point Lighthouse** (33439 County Rte. 6, 315/654-3450, www.hiusa.org/capevincent, July 1-Sept. 15, $25 per night in dorms) is a Hosteling International property offering 21 dormitory-style beds in single-sex rooms; family rooms also are available.

The boxy, brick **Roxy Hotel** (Broadway and Market St., 315/654-2456, www.theroxy-hotel.com, $80) has operated continuously since 1894, with a brief break for renovations in 2011. Downstairs, an Irish pub offers beer and food; upstairs are 10 simple but adequate guest rooms.

CLAYTON

One of the most interesting villages along the St. Lawrence, Clayton contains four museums and the Thousand Islands Inn, where Thousand Island salad dressing was invented. The town spreads along the riverfront, with lots of park benches ideal for watching the swift current slide by. All along Riverside Drive stand sturdy brick storefronts, built in the late 1800s. An exception to the functional brick retail spaces is **Simon Johnston House,** a clapboard Italianate home with a widow's walk and decorative eaves, located at the corner of Riverside Drive and Merrick Street.

Settled in 1822, Clayton soon developed into a major shipbuilding center and steamboat port. The St. Lawrence skiff, known for its sleekness and beauty, was first constructed here by Xavier Colon in 1868, and the 900-passenger *St. Lawrence,* the largest steamboat ever made, was built in the 1890s. During World War I, the Clayton shipyards produced submarine chasers and pontoon boats.

Tourists began frequenting Clayton in the late 1800s. Most came to fish and boat, and they stayed in huge wooden hotels—which have since burned down—along the waterfront. During Clayton's heyday, five express trains arrived here daily from New York City, and one hotel was equipped with a direct line to the New York Stock Exchange. Some

vacationers even came during the winter, to ice-fish and watch the horse races run on the frozen St. Lawrence River.

Walking tour maps of the town are available at **Clayton Chamber of Commerce** (517 Riverside Dr., 315/686-3771, www.1000islands-clayton.com, July-Sept. daily 9am-5pm, Oct.-June Mon.-Fri. 9am-4pm).

Antique Boat Museum

Appropriately enough, Clayton has the finest collection of antique wooden boats in America. Among them are canoes, sailboats, launches, race boats, runabouts, and, of course, the famed *St. Lawrence* skiff. The gleaming boats, most built of highly polished woods and brass, are housed at the **Antique Boat Museum** (750 Mary St., 315/686-4104, www.abm.org, hours and admission vary seasonally) in a former lumberyard on the edge of town. There are over 300 vessels in all, spread out over eight buildings, along with a boatbuilding shop, almost 300 inboard and outboard motors, and thousands of nautical artifacts. The museum also contains extensive historical exhibits.

Thousand Islands Museum

Inside the eclectic **Thousand Islands Museum** (312 James St., 315/686-5794, www.timuseum. org, hours vary seasonally, donations accepted), you'll find the Muskie Hall of Fame, devoted to the region's most prized fish, and an enormous collection of hand-carved decoys, a popular North Country folk art. According to the exhibit, one riverman claims to have carved over 1,000 decoys, another about 5,000. Also on-site are recreated turn-of-the-century storefronts, including a general store, millinery shop, law office, and old country kitchen.

Thousand Islands Arts Center

The **Thousand Islands Arts Center** (314 John St., 315/686-4123, www.tiartscenter.org, Mon.-Fri. 9am-5pm, Sat. 10am-4pm) began its life as the Handweaving Museum, but its name, mission, collection, and schedule of events and workshops expanded in 2009 to reflect a more diverse range of arts. Handwoven

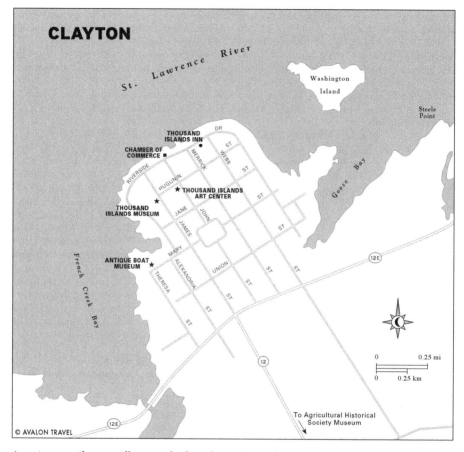

CLAYTON

St. Lawrence River

Washington Island

Steele Point

THOUSAND ISLANDS INN

CHAMBER OF COMMERCE

★ THOUSAND ISLANDS ART CENTER

THOUSAND ISLANDS MUSEUM

ANTIQUE BOAT MUSEUM ★

Goose Bay

French Creek Bay

MERRICK
WEBB
RIVERSIDE
HUGUNIN
JANE
JAMES
JOHN
MARY
ALEXANDRIA
THERESA
UNION
DR
ST
ST
ST
ST
ST
ST
ST
ST
ST
ST
ST
ST
ST

12E
12
12E

0   0.25 mi
0   0.25 km

To Agricultural Historical Society Museum

© AVALON TRAVEL

American textiles are still a specialty here, but photographs and other arts are exhibited and taught here as well.

Events

One of the region's most popular events, sponsored by the Antique Boat Museum, is the resplendent **Antique Boat Show and Auction** (315/686-3771), held every August for nearly 50 years. The **Decoy and Wildlife Art Show** (315/686-3771), attracting over 200 exhibitors, is held in the Clayton Arena in mid-July.

Accommodations and Camping

The 1897 **(Thousand Islands Inn** (335 Riverside Dr., 315/686-3030, www.1000-islands.com/inn, $85-170) is the last of the great old hotels that once lined Clayton. Significantly smaller than it was in its heyday, it offers 13 modern guest rooms, some overlooking the river. The historic restaurant where Thousand Island dressing was invented is downstairs.

Campsites are available at 165-site **Cedar Point State Park** (36661 Cedar Point State Park Dr., 315/654-2522, reservations 800/456-2267, www.nysparks.com/parks/21) and at three island campgrounds accessible only by boat.

Vacationing onboard houseboats is a popular activity in the Thousand Islands, and numerous houseboat-rental companies once lined the New York side of the St. Lawrence. Today, visitors who want to rent a houseboat will have to cross to the Canadian side, as insurance costs have made houseboat rentals cost-prohibitive for U.S. companies. No boating experience is necessary to rent a houseboat, as instruction is provided. Reservations should be made well in advance.

Food

At **Thousands Islands Inn** (355 Riverside Dr., 315/686-3030, $22), you'll find a comfortable, old-fashioned restaurant serving everything from steak and fish to pasta. For sale are bottles of "Original Thousand Island Salad Dressing," created here in the early 1900s by Sophia LaLonde.

Koffee Kove (220 James St., 315/686-2472, daily 6am-8pm) is known for its chili and homemade breads.

The chef-owned **Clipper Inn** (126 State St., 315/686-3842, www.clipperinn.com, Wed.-Sun. 5pm-close, $22) is a local favorite, serving lots of seafood in an upscale yet casual setting.

ALEXANDRIA BAY

About 10 miles northeast of Clayton is Alexandria Bay, a busy tourist village where you'll find all sorts of 1950s-era attractions, including miniature golf courses, junior speedways, kitschy souvenir shops, and mom-and-pop motels.

But for all its summertime hustle and bustle, Alexandria Bay has a permanent population of just 1,116 and a laid-back, down-home charm. The village centers around its waterfront, where a few narrow streets are crowded with tiny shops and restaurants. Teenagers strut their stuff in front of an amusement arcade, while twentysomethings exchange glances outside a boisterous bar.

Alexandria Bay was a popular tourist resort and steamboat stop throughout the late 1800s and early 1900s. Millionaires built second homes on the islands across from the village, while hotels went up along the shore.

Today, Alexandria Bay is the main port for touring the Thousand Islands. Excursion boats dock at weathered piers at both ends of the village. For more information on the area, stop into the **Alexandria Bay Chamber of Commerce** (7 Market St., 315/482-9531, www.visitalexbay.org, daily 9am-5pm, with extended hours in July-Aug.).

◖ Boldt Castle

Looming over Heart Island, across from Alexandria Bay, is a 127-room replica of a Rhineland castle. **Boldt Castle** (Heart Island, 315/482-2501, www.boldtcastle.com, hours vary seasonally, adults $11, children 6-12 $7, plus the cost of the boat ride over) was built by George Boldt, who came to the United States from Prussia in the 1860s. The son of poor parents, Boldt had tremendous industry and skill, and eventually became the most successful hotel magnate in the country. Both the Waldorf Astoria in New York City and the Bellevue Stratford in Philadelphia were his.

Boldt was deeply in love with his wife, Louise, and built the castle around the turn of the 20th century as a symbol of his love for her. The castle was to be their summer home, and he employed the finest craftspeople, instructing them to embellish the building with hearts wherever they could. Boldt even had the island reshaped into the form of a heart.

Then in 1904, when the castle was 80 percent complete, Louise passed away. Boldt sent a telegram to the construction crew to stop work immediately, and never set foot on the island again. The castle was abandoned and allowed to deteriorate.

Finally, in 1977, the Thousand Islands Bridge Authority bought Boldt Castle, partially rehabilitated it, and introduced it to the tourist trade. Today, hundreds of visitors traipse through it daily, but all the activity in the world can't erase the castle's haunted, wildly romantic feel. In the former ballroom, exhibits explain the castle's history.

A shuttle boat operates from the castle to the **Boldt Yacht House,** perched on a separate island nearby. Completed before Louise's death, the boathouse contains three original spit-and-polish boats and restored living quarters furnished with handsome antiques.

Excursion Boats

The only way to reach Boldt Island, as well as the other 1,800-plus islands in the St. Lawrence River, is by boat. Several boat companies offer tours, including **Uncle Sam's Boat Tours** (315/482-2611, www.usboattours.com), whose huge replica paddle boats dock at the eastern end of James Street. Uncle Sam's features an hourly **shuttle service** (adults $8, children 4-12 $4.50) to Boldt Castle that allows visitors to stay as long as they like, as well as various sightseeing and dining cruises.

Cornwall Brothers Store and Museum

Evidence of Alexandria Bay's early 20th-century heyday can be found at **Cornwall Brothers Store and Museum** (36 Market St., 315/482-4586, www.alexandriahistorical.com, May-Sept. days vary 9am-5pm). Originally owned by the town's founder, Azariah Walton, the building is now part museum, part recreated general store. Up front, choose from a nice selection of penny candy, vintage postcards, handicrafts, and books; in the back are historic photographs and artifacts.

Wellesley Island State Park

To reach Wellesley Island and **Wellesley Island State Park** (44927 Cross Island Rd., Fineview, 315/482-2722, www.nysparks.com/parks/52, $8 parking) you must travel over the **Thousand Islands International Bridge,** a slim suspension expanse that seems to lead straight up into the sky. Built in 1938, the bridge extends over five spans and stretches seven miles.

At the end of the first span lies the 2,636-acre state park, featuring hiking trails, swimming beaches, a campground, nine-hole golf course, playground, and great views of the river. Covering 600 acres of the park is the **Minna Anthony Common Nature Center** (44927 Cross Island Rd., 315/482-2479, daily 10am-4pm, extended hours in summer, free), which includes both a museum and a wildlife

sanctuary laced with trails. Live fish and reptiles, mounted birds, and an observation beehive are in the museum.

Thousand Island Park

South of the state park, at the very tip of Wellesley Island, lies **Thousand Island Park** (Wellesley Island, 315/482-2576, www.tiparkcorp.com), a quiet community filled with hundreds of wooden Victorian homes painted in luscious ice-cream pastels. Ornate carvings, shingled roofs, porches, turrets, and gables abound.

On the National Register of Historic Places, the park is largely privately owned but visitors are welcome. The community has its own movie theater, post office, library, and playground.

Accommodations and Camping

Campsites are available at the 73-site **Grass Point State Park** (42247 Grassy Point Rd., 315/686-4472, reservations 800/456-2267, www.nysparks.com/parks/139) and the 434-site **Wellesley Island State Park** (Wellesley Island, 315/482-2722, reservations 800/456-2267, www.nysparks.com/parks/52).

Capt. Thomson's (45 James St., 315/482-9961, www.captthomsons.com, $79-139) contains 68 standard rooms, some with balconies overlooking the river. **Hart House Inn Bed and Breakfast** (21979 Club Rd., 315/482-5683, www.harthouseinn.com, $95-325) served as the 1000 Island Golf Club and now offers peaceful guest rooms with fireplaces, whirlpools, and canopy beds, along with a hearty local breakfast.

 Riveredge Resort (17 Holland St., 315/482-9917, www.riveredge.com, $72-198) features views of the river and Boldt Castle. The hotel's rooms and suites are spacious and well-appointed; on-site are a health spa, indoor and outdoor pools, and a restaurant and lounge.

The sleek **Bonnie Castle** (31 Holland St., 315/482-4511, www.bonniecastle.com, $180-290 d) is the region's largest resort, equipped with 129 rooms and suites, a conference center, private beach, swimming pools, tennis courts, nightclub, miniature golf courses, and restaurants.

Food

Numerous casual restaurants can be found on James and Market Streets downtown. Among them is lively **Dockside Pub** (17 Market St., 315/482-9849), serving sandwiches, soups, and pizza in a setting near the water.

Hidden waterfront hot spot **Foxy's** (18187 Reed Point Rd., Fishers Landing, between Clayton and Alexandria Bay, 315/686-3781) is a small family-run eatery with great lobster bisque and an even better view of the sunset.

Historic **Admiral's Inn** (20 James St., 315/482-4469, $16) features a comfortable bar to one side, several cheery dining rooms to the other. Sandwiches and salads are offered at lunch, while dinner entrées include prime rib and fresh seafood.

The best restaurant in town is **Jacques Cartier Dining Room** (17 Holland St., 315/482-9917, www.riveredge.com, $32) in the Riveredge Resort. On the menu is creative American and French cuisine. The dining room offers fine views of Boldt Castle.

OGDENSBURG

The oldest settlement in northern New York, established in 1749, Ogdensburg is a busy port and industrial town at the juncture of the Oswegatchie and St. Lawrence Rivers. Downtown, **Greenbelt Riverfront Park** runs along the St. Lawrence, dotted with historical plaques that detail the War of 1812 Battle of Ogdensburg. A few blocks south of the park is the town's foremost visitor attraction: the Frederic Remington Art Museum.

Frederic Remington Art Museum

Artist Frederic Remington (1861-1909), best known for his paintings and bronzes of the American West, was born in the northernmost reaches of New York State. In his youth he made a total of 18 trips out West, collecting information and taking photographs that he would later use in his studio in New Rochelle,

NY, to create his masterpieces. Remington never lived in Ogdensburg, but was born and is buried in nearby Canton. His wife moved to Ogdensburg after his death.

Housed in an imposing 1810 mansion, **Frederic Remington Art Museum** (303 Washington St., 315/393-2425, www.fredericremington.org, May 15-Oct. 15 Mon.-Sat. 10am-5pm and Sun. 1pm-5pm, Oct. 16-May 14 Wed.-Sat. 11am-5pm and Sun. 1pm-5pm, adults $9, students and seniors $8, children under 15 $2-7) contains the largest single Remington collection in the United States. On display are scores of oil paintings, watercolors, drawings, illustrations, and bronzes, including many small and relatively unknown gems. One room is filled with watercolors depicting the Adirondacks, another with a reproduction of Remington's studio. The most valuable Remingtons are kept in a locked gallery that is only open during guided tours, scheduled regularly throughout the day.

CANTON

About 20 miles east of Ogdensburg lies Canton, artist Frederic Remington's birthplace. Settled by Vermonters in the early 1800s, Canton today is a busy small town (pop. 6,669), best known as the home of St. Lawrence University.

TAUNY Center and North Country Folkstore

It's worth a detour to Canton to visit **TAUNY Center and North Country Folkstore** (53 Main St., 315/386-4289, www.tauny.org, Tues.-Fri. 10am-5pm, Sat. 10am-4pm, donation), a unique arts gallery and gift shop located in a historic downtown building. North Country Folkstore offers buyable art made through traditional practices in the region. TAUNY (Traditional Arts in Upstate New York) Center exhibits detail specific elements of local life, and a portrait gallery of North Country Heritage Award winners rounds out the facility, which also offers hands-on demonstrations and lectures by skilled artisans. Exhibits in the past have highlighted such subjects as St. Lawrence River fishing arts,

THERE ARE A THOUSAND STORIES IN THE THOUSAND ISLANDS

The 1,864 islands of the Thousand Islands laze in the deep blue St. Lawrence River like a "drunken doodle made by an addled cartographer," as one observer once said. Each and every one tells a story.

- The largest of the islands is **Wolfe Island.** The smallest is Tom Thumb. The only artificial island, **Longue Vue Island,** was formed by filling in the area between two shoals. As the story goes, Longue Vue was created by a doting husband who wanted to build a summer home for his wife. When he couldn't find a single island that suited her, he had one built, and then added a luxurious mansion atop it. His wife then ran off with another man.

- Devil's Oven on **Devil's Island** was the 1838 refuge of Canadian patriot Bill Johnston. After an aborted attempt to wrest Canada from the British Empire, Johnston hid out in the cave for nearly a year before surrendering to the authorities. He was later pardoned and appointed a lighthouse keeper.

- The **Price is Right Island** was given away in 1964 by Bill Cullen on *The Price is Right* TV game show. **Deer Island** is owned by the Skull and Bones Society of Yale University.

Abbie Hoffman lived incognito—under the name Barry Freed—on **Wellesley Island** after jumping bail on cocaine charges in 1974.

- **Florence Island,** Arthur Godfrey's isle, was given to him as a gift by the Thousand Islands Bridge Authority in return for free advertising. Godfrey sang the song "Florence on the St. Lawrence."

- **Grindstone Island** was the site of the last existing one-room schoolhouse in New York State, in use until 1989.

- **Ash Island** has its own private railroad line running from the boathouse to the main house on the cliff.

- George Pullman of Pullman Car fame once owned **Pullman Island** and played frequent host to President Ulysses S. Grant.

- **Calumet Island** was once the property of Charles Emery, president of the American Tobacco Company.

- **Picton Island** was owned by M. Heineman, originator of Buster Brown Shoes.

- **Oppawaka Island** was owned by J.H. Heinz of Heinz 57 fame.

Mohawk tourist arts, quilts and quilting bees, and Old Order Amish crafts. Thoughtfully laid out displays offer plenty of background information and photographs.

The gallery is also a good place to find out about folk arts events. Storytelling still thrives in the North Country, and there are occasional traditional music concerts and dance fests in the area.

Silas Wright Museum

Run by the St. Lawrence County Historical Association, the columned Greek Revival **Silas Wright Museum** (3 E. Main St., 315/386-8133, Tues.-Thurs. and Sat. noon-4pm, Fri. noon-8pm, donations welcome) once belonged to U.S. senator and New York governor Silas

Wright. Regarded as an honest and intelligent man, Wright was so respected by his neighbors that he won his first election to the state senate in 1823 by 199 votes to one; legend has it that he himself cast the one dissenting vote. The first floor of the house has been restored to its 1830-50 period appearance, while upstairs are local history exhibits. St. Lawrence County is one of the largest and least populated counties east of the Mississippi.

MASSENA

The main reason to make a stop in the small industrial city of Massena is to get a good look at the giant **St. Lawrence Seaway,** which connects the Atlantic Ocean with the Great Lakes. A joint project of the United States and

Canada, the Seaway can accommodate ships up to 730 feet long and 76 feet wide. The public works project was formally dedicated on June 26, 1959 by Queen Elizabeth II and President Eisenhower.

Dwight D. Eisenhower Lock

Atop the long, spare **Dwight D. Eisenhower Lock** (Barnhart Island Rd., off Rte. 37, 315/764-3200) is a viewing deck from which you can watch ships being raised or lowered 42 feet as they pass through the Seaway. The process takes about 10 minutes and displaces 22 million gallons of water. Ships pass through regularly, except in the winter when the St. Lawrence freezes over, but the viewing deck is only open June-September. Below the lock, a small **interpretive center** (315/769-2049, June-Sept. daily 9am-9pm) offers exhibits and a short film.

Robert Moses State Park and Campground

Adjoining the Power Project, **Robert Moses State Park** (19 Robinson Bay Rd., 315/769-8663, camping reservations 800/456-2267, www.nysparks.com/parks/51) is spread across the mainland and Barnhart Island. It is accessible through a tunnel beneath Eisenhower Lock and includes a swimming beach, bathhouse, boat rentals, picnic tables, playground, and great views of the river. The park also offers a 212-site campground.

AKWESASNE

At the confluence of the St. Regis and St. Lawrence Rivers lies the St. Regis Indian Reservation, or Akwesasne (the name means "Where the Ruffed Grouse Drums"). Gas stations selling tax-free gasoline, and mock tepees selling souvenirs line the roadsides. Signs along Route 37 include: This Is Indian Land; Private Property; No FBI, IRS, or Other Agencies.

Akwesasne is home to about 12,000 residents. The reservation straddles the St. Lawrence Seaway and the United States/Canadian border, and includes several islands.

In Hogansburg, about 10 miles east of Massena, is the large and well laid out **Akwesasne Museum** (321 Rte. 37, 518/358-2240 or 518/358-2461, www.akwesasneculturalcenter.org, hours vary seasonally, adults $2, children 5-16 $1), housed in a big brown building that's also home to the Akwesasne Cultural Center and Library. The museum covers an entire floor and contains an outstanding collection of medicine masks, wampum belts, lacrosse sticks, carved cradle boards, water drums, Bibles written in the Mohawk language, beadwork, quillwork, modern artwork, historical photographs, and basketry.

Especially striking are the photography and basket exhibits. The photographs date back to the 1920s and depict a prosperous, pre-Depression Mohawk community bustling with shiny cars, sturdy baby prams, women in white dresses, and men in hats. The basket exhibit contains everything from a wedding basket, which looks just like a cake, to a thimble basket.

East of the museum is **Akwesasne Mohawk Casino** (873 Rte. 37, 877/99-CASINO, www.mohawkcasino.com, daily 24 hours). Opened in spring 1999, the casino offers blackjack, craps, and roulette tables, and hundreds of video lottery terminals.

Information and Services

The **Finger Lakes Tourism Alliance** (309 Lake St., Penn Yan, 315/536-7488, www.fingerlakes.org) is a good central information source for the entire region.

Contact **Finger Lakes Wine Country Tourism Marketing Association** (1 W. Market St., Corning, 607/936-0706, www.fingerlakeswinecountry.com) for information about grape-growing regions around Keuka, Seneca, and Cayuga Lakes. Each of the lakes also has a "wine trail" website: www.keukawinetrail.com, www.senecalakewine.com, and www.cayugawinetrail.com. Contact **The Landmark Society of Western New York** (585/546-7029, www.landmarksociety.org) for walking tours in Rochester. For self-guided tours, download maps on their website.

Several B&B registries operate in the Finger Lakes. Among them are **Finger Lakes B&B Association** (www.flbba.org), **B&B Association of Greater Ithaca** (800/806-4406, www.bbithaca.com), and B&B's of Skaneateles (www.bbskaneateles.com).

Many counties, cities, and towns have their own visitor information centers. Most are open Monday-Friday 9am-5pm.

* **Greater Syracuse Convention and Visitors Bureau** (572 S. Salina St., Syracuse, 315/470-1910, www.visitsyracuse.org)

* **Skaneateles Area Chamber of Commerce** (22 Jordan St., Skaneateles, 315/685-0552, www.skaneateles.com)

* **Cayuga County Office of Tourism** (131 Genesee St., Auburn, 800/499-9615, www.tourcayuga.com)

* **Seneca County Chamber of Commerce** (2020 Rtes. 5 and 20 W., Seneca Falls, 800/732-1848, www.fingerlakescentral.com)

* **Ithaca/Tompkins County Convention and Visitors Bureau** (904 E. Shore Dr., Ithaca, 607/272-1313, www.visitithaca.com)

* **Geneva Area Chamber of Commerce** (1 Franklin Sq., Geneva, 315/789-1776, www.genevany.com)

* **Finger Lakes Visitors Connection** (25 Gorham St., Canandaigua, 877/386-4669, www.visitfingerlakes.com)

* **Clifton Springs Chamber of Commerce** (2 E. Main St., Clifton Springs, 315/462-8200, www.cliftonspringschamber.com)

* **Victor Chamber of Commerce** (37 E. Main St., Victor, 585/742-1476, www.victorchamber.com)

* **Phelps Chamber of Commerce** (116 Main St., Phelps, 315/548-5481, www.phelpsny.com)

* **Steuben County Conference & Visitors Bureau** (1 W. Market St., Ste. 201, Corning, 607/936-6544, www.corningfingerlakes.com)

* **Corning Area Chamber of Commerce** (1 W. Market St., Corning, 607/936-4686, www.corningny.com)

* **Canandaigua Chamber of Commerce** (113 S. Main St., Canandaigua, 585/394-4400, www.canandaiguachamber.com)

* **Cortland County Convention and Visitors' Bureau** (37 Church St., Cortland, 607/753-8463, www.experiencecortland.com)

* **Wayne County Tourism** (9 Pearl St., Lyons, 800/527-6510, www.waynecountytourism.com)

* **Watkins Glen Area Chamber of Commerce** (214 N. Franklin St., Watkins Glen, 607/535-4300, www.watkinsglenchamber.com)

* **VisitRochester** (45 East Ave., Ste. 400, 585/279-8300, www.visitrochester.com)

* **Thousand Islands Regional Tourism Development Corporation** (Box 709 Wellesley Island, 315/482-2520, www.visit1000islands.com)

Getting There and Around

Syracuse Hancock International Airport (www.syrairport.org) is serviced by **AirCanada** (888/247-2262), **Allegiant** (702/505-8888), **American Airlines** (800/433-7300), **Delta** (800/221-1212), **JetBlue** (800/538-2583), **United** (800/241-6522), and **USAirways** (800/428-4322). Delta, United, and USAirways also service **Ithaca Tompkins Regional Airport** (www.flyithaca.com). Allegiant, Delta, and USAirways fly into and out of **Elmira-Corning Regional Airport** (www.ecairport. com). AirCanada, American Airlines, Delta, JetBlue, **Southwest** (800/435-9792), United, and USAirways service **Greater Rochester International Airport** (www2.monroecounty. gov/airport-index.php).

A taxi ride from any of these airports to their respective downtowns costs $20-30.

Amtrak (800/872-7245, www.amtrak.com) travels to Syracuse and Rochester. **Greyhound** (800/231-2222, www.greyhound.com) and **New York State Trailways** (800/295-5555 or 800/776-7548) provide bus service throughout the region.

By far the best way to explore the Finger Lakes and Thousand Islands is by car.

MAP SYMBOLS

▭▭▭ Expressway	**C**	Highlight	✗	Airfield	⚲	Golf Course
▭▭▭ Primary Road	○	City/Town	✗	Airport	**P**	Parking Area
▭▭▭ Secondary Road	◉	State Capital	▲	Mountain	⛰	Archaeological Site
▭▭▭ Unpaved Road	⊛	National Capital	✛	Unique Natural Feature	♠	Church
------ Trail	★	Point of Interest			🔋	Gas Station
·········· Ferry	•	Accommodation	🦅	Waterfall	◌	Glacier
-·-·-·- Railroad	▼	Restaurant/Bar	⚑	Park	🗺	Mangrove
▭▭▭ Pedestrian Walkway	▪	Other Location	❶	Trailhead	▨	Reef
⅏ Stairs	Λ	Campground	⛷	Skiing Area	▭	Swamp

CONVERSION TABLES

°C = (°F - 32) / 1.8
°F = (°C x 1.8) + 32
1 inch = 2.54 centimeters (cm)
1 foot = 0.304 meters (m)
1 yard = 0.914 meters
1 mile = 1.6093 kilometers (km)
1 km = 0.6214 miles
1 fathom = 1.8288 m
1 chain = 20.1168 m
1 furlong = 201.168 m
1 acre = 0.4047 hectares
1 sq km = 100 hectares
1 sq mile = 2.59 square km
1 ounce = 28.35 grams
1 pound = 0.4536 kilograms
1 short ton = 0.90718 metric ton
1 short ton = 2,000 pounds
1 long ton = 1.016 metric tons
1 long ton = 2,240 pounds
1 metric ton = 1,000 kilograms
1 quart = 0.94635 liters
1 US gallon = 3.7854 liters
1 Imperial gallon = 4.5459 liters
1 nautical mile = 1.852 km

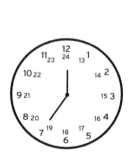

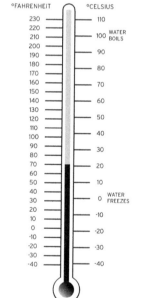

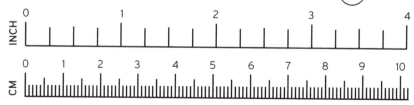

MOON SPOTLIGHT FINGER LAKES
Avalon Travel
a member of the Perseus Books Group
1700 Fourth Street
Berkeley, CA 94710, USA
www.moon.com

Editor: Kevin McLain
Series Manager: Kathryn Ettinger
Copy Editor: Naomi Adler Dancis
Graphics and Production Coordinator: Lucie Ericksen
Cover Design: Faceout Studios, Charles Brock
Moon Logo: Tim McGrath
Map Editor: Mike Morgenfeld
Cartographer: Stephanie Poulain
Proofreader: Mindy Cooper

ISBN-13: 978-1-61238-792-5

ABOUT THE AUTHOR

Julie Schwietert Collazo

Like most New Yorkers, Julie Schwietert Collazo took a long time to discover the state beyond "the city so nice, they named it twice." When she finally started exploring beyond the five boroughs while on assignment for the BBC, she discovered just how much of America's history can be traced back to New York. She also realized how diverse the state is, both culturally and geographically. From the Amish country in western New York to the Thousand Islands, New York State has so much for travelers to discover.

Together, Julie and her husband, Cuban-born photographer Francisco Collazo, have published work in *TIME, Discover, National Geographic Traveler, Scientific American,* and numerous other publications. They live in Long Island City with their two children, who both got their passports at one month of age and are accustomed to being packed up and buckled into the seat of a car, plane, or train at a moment's notice.

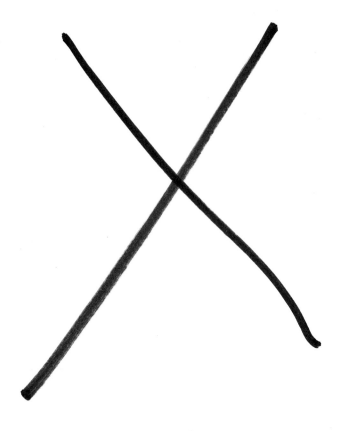

CPSIA information can be obtained at www.ICGtesting.com
Printed in the USA
LVOW04s0310220814

400250LV00011B/38/P

9 781612 387925